# Tack:
## How to Choose it and Use it

# Tack:
# How to Choose it and Use it

Carolyn Henderson

SWAN·HILL
PRESS

# Dedication

For my father, Cyril Gilbert, with love and thanks.

First published in the UK in 1996
by Swan Hill Press, an imprint of Airlife Publishing Ltd

**British Library Cataloguing in Publication Data**
A catalogue record for this book
is available from the British Library

ISBN 1 85310 596 1

Photographs by John Henderson

Typeset by Hewer Text Composition Services, Edinburgh
Printed in England by Butler & Tanner Ltd, Frome and London

**Swan Hill Press**
an imprint of Airlife Publishing Ltd
101 Longden Road, Shrewsbury SY3 9EB England

# Contents

# Acknowledgements

A lot of people have added to my knowledge and/or provoked thought on the subjects covered in this book. They will not necessarily all agree with every sentiment expressed in it, but thanks are due to: Sara Barnes, David and Robin Coleman, Pat Crawford, Julia Forsyth, Malan Goddard, Kent Lyndon-Dykes, Barry and Lorna Richardson, Lynn Russell, Tony Russell, Nick Ward, Liz Wyatt and Tracey Lloyd.

# Chapter 1
## Making the Right Choice

Choosing and using the right tack and equipment is a vital skill for anyone who rides or looks after horses and ponies. Mistakes are expensive – and not just in terms of hard cash. The safety and comfort of both you and your horse depend on you getting it right; if the stitching on a rein, girth or stirrup leather breaks whilst you are riding, you have the ingredients for a nasty accident.

Whatever job a horse does, whether he is a top competition animal or a family hack, he has to be comfortable if he is to do it to the best of his ability. On the most basic level, this means that his tack must be fitted and adjusted correctly, his rugs must be the right size and well designed so they stay in place, and he must wear the right protective equipment if he travels in a horsebox or trailer.

That might sound so obvious that it is hardly worth stating. But go to any show or competition and you will see unhappy horses ridden by equally unhappy owners; some animals may try and open their mouths wide to resist the bit, while others go with their heads in the air and/or with stiff backs. There can be all sorts of reasons for this, but badly fitting tack is one of the commonest.

For instance, many riders use bits that are too big for their horses' mouths and then compound the error by adjusting them too low. When a horse bitted this way attempts to evade the discomfort by opening his mouth or putting his tongue over the mouthpiece, the rider then fastens his mouth shut with some type of drop noseband to try and solve the 'problem'.

Problems do not arise only at novice level. A leading saddle-maker and fitter with a wide knowledge of horse anatomy recently attended a prestigious national dressage competition purely to assess standards of saddle fit. She found that only about a third of the combinations met her criteria, yet these were the élite. If their horses could perform while they were being pinched, rubbed or restricted by their saddles, how much more could they achieve when fitted with and ridden in saddles that helped rather than hindered their movement?

Even seemingly innocuous things like rugs can cause long-term damage. If the rug pulls down across the withers and spine – or even worse, is kept in place with a tight surcingle or badly fitting roller – it can cause just as many problems as an ill-fitting saddle. Likewise, bandages put on too tight can damage tendons and tails.

So how do you make sure that you and your horse are on the right tack? The obvious answer is to get expert advice, but finding it is sometimes easier said than done. When it comes to the bottom line, you are responsible for your horse's comfort and the safety of you both. It is therefore up to you to assess what to use and how to use it.

That is where this book comes in. It deals with the basic equipment that every rider and owner has to use, and also the specialist tack that individual problems may tempt you to try, such as training aids. It explains how things work when fitted and used the correct way – and tries to minimise the risk of things going wrong.

Obviously there are times when you will need expert help, such as when buying a new saddle. But even then, you have to take a fair amount of responsibility yourself: some saddlers are craftsmen, not fitting experts, and not everyone who sells saddles knows how to fit them. The relative few who combine saddlery skills with a knowledge of equine anatomy and have the ability to assess horse and rider together are much in demand – and worth every penny they charge.

You will also need to refine your skills in assessing your horse or pony's conformation and movement, and use these observations in choosing, and possibly changing, the equipment you use. Horses, like people, do not come in standard shapes and sizes. There is no such thing as a magic wand (or bit, or gadget) that will solve your schooling problems – but a change of tack and equipment can often produce amazing results.

On the other hand, sometimes you may have to accept that your horse is limited by his conformation and that, while correct schooling will do a lot of good and the right tack will help you produce the best possible results, his shape may prevent him from achieving the perfection you aim for. For instance, a horse who has a ewe neck, which looks as if it has been set on to his body upside down, will find it hard to flex and come on to the bit.

If you think the horse might have a soundness problem, however slight, always start by asking your vet's advice; your horse might be more supple on one rein than the other because of his natural way of going – just as we are usually right-handed or left-handed – but he might be compensating for discomfort or injury.

It takes a trained eye to spot the very slight deviations from perfect gait and carriage, but you know – or should know – your own horse. If something feels wrong, tell your vet, even if everyone else thinks you are worrying over nothing.

For instance, no one but me thought one of my horses was 'wrong'; common explanations were that he was 'bridle halting', restricting his gait in order to avoid working from behind into the rider's hand, or that I was paranoid! When the horse was examined and scanned at our veterinary practice's diagnostic centre, it turned out that he had a tilted pelvis. He was one tenth lame on a hindleg; hindleg lameness is more difficult for the average eye to see, and this was so slight that it compounded the difficulty. (The degree of lameness is expressed in tenths: one tenth lame is very hard for an untrained eye to recognise, while four or five tenths is easy to see.)

We know that the horse did not have a fall while being ridden, which is a common cause of injuries of this kind, but apparently it could have happened in all sorts of ways

– perhaps by him coming to an abrupt halt when playing in the field, or through getting cast in his stable during the night without anyone realising it. If I had carried on working and jumping him as normal, he would have been in constant pain.

## Assessing your horse

In order to decide what sort of tack and equipment is right for your horse, you need to start by taking a long, hard look at his conformation, muscle development and movement. If you find this difficult, ask someone whose opinion you respect to help. Do not feel stupid if you cannot assess your own horse as easily as you can someone else's; many people are so fond of their horses that they refuse to accept that they have any faults – or alternatively, are having such a terrible time with them that they can only think of the bad points.

The aim is not to decide if the horse will win prizes in the show ring, so this is not a guide to ideal conformation. Even so, you need to keep a blueprint in your mind so you

*A horse's conformation and state of maturity will affect how easy or difficult it is to fit tack, especially saddles. This four-year-old Irish Draught cross Thoroughbred is still growing and is higher behind than in front; he is also a bit straight in the shoulder. Both factors make it hard to fit conventional saddles, though the problems were overcome by using a Reactorpanel saddle, as shown on the cover of this book.*

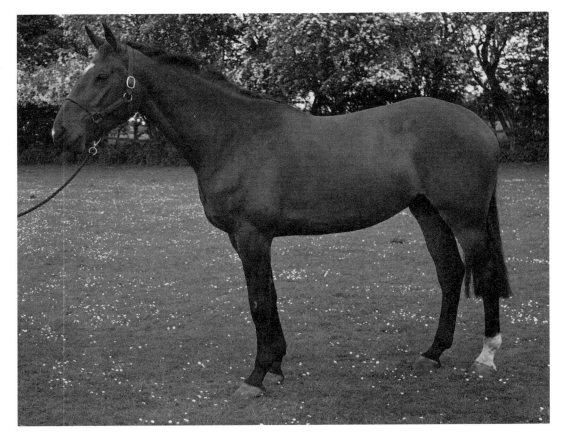

*Compare him with this horse, of the same age and breeding. Skipper has a good sloping shoulder and was easy to fit correctly. However, because he has a short mouth he is uncomfortable in a bit with a thick mouthpiece and prefers a thinner snaffle or one with a French link mouthpiece.*

can recognise variations from it, identify the problems they may cause in the way the horse goes and choose the tack and equipment that might help you to make improvements. (For an in-depth look at conformation, see *Showing to Win* by Carolyn Henderson and Lynn Russell, published by Swan Hill Press.)

Your assessment is not a final summing up. It is something you need to do regularly, because as a horse changes shape and condition so does the fit of your saddle and rugs. Spring grass may add to his weight and correct work will build up his muscles.

First of all, does the horse 'fill your eye' and present a harmonious picture of flowing lines, or is there something that detracts from the symmetry? Sometimes a horse will look as if its front and back ends should belong to two different animals. You have to accept that a young horse will go through one or more 'ugly duckling' stages before it hopefully turns into a swan, but you should be able to look at the three-year-old and predict what he will be like when he fills out and matures.

The growing youngster will often go through stages when he is higher behind than in front, but the mature horse who is croup high will need careful schooling to overcome his natural tendency to go on his forehand – after all, he is built downhill. His saddle will need to be fitted with extra care. You will also need to be choosy about his rugs; poorly designed ones may pull across his withers, which in time can do as much damage as a badly fitting saddle.

The horse who has a big front but is weak behind will also need expert saddle-fitting. The saddle will tend to slip back on both this horse and the herring-gutted animal – the one who always looks 'run up' like a greyhound.

## Back, withers and shoulders

Run your fingers along each side of your horse's back, covering the saddle area and just behind it. Use firm but not rough pressure – do not dig in with your fingers. The idea is to discover any areas that are sore or tense, not to provoke a reaction at any cost – if someone dug you in the back, you would flinch whether you were sore or not, and the same applies to horses. Do his muscles feel relaxed, do they have a certain amount of 'give', or are there areas which are noticeably tight?

*This three-year-old Thoroughbred mare, photographed when she came out of racing, has white hairs on her prominent withers. This is a sign that she has been rubbed by a badly fitting saddle or rug.*

Watch the horse's reactions whilst you are doing this. Is he happy to be handled in this way, or does he show signs of discomfort? These could include putting his head up or bobbing it up and down, laying his ears back or trying to nip you.

Follow the same procedure on either side of the withers, where muscles can be damaged by a saddle with an incorrect tree width. Examine the withers themselves, too. Rubs and sores are an obvious giveaway; white hair is a sign of previous damage from badly fitting rugs, rollers or saddles.

If you notice any reactions that could be a sign of discomfort, stop riding him and ask your vet to check him. The vet will hopefully be able to identify the problem and help you put it right, but it is important to identify the underlying cause. The root of the problem may be an ill-fitting saddle, but the scenario may be more complicated, especially if accompanied by variations in gait such as a shortened stride.

Think about how you react if you have a pain in, say, your left ankle. You adjust the way you carry yourself and the way you move to take as much stress as possible off the affected area. Your horse will do the same, but with the added burden of a saddle and rider. If he is trying to move this combined weight to one side, it will have a knock-on effect on the fit of your saddle.

Stand behind the horse and look at his muscle development. Is he symmetrical, or is his croup, quarters or stifle noticeably more wasted on one side than the other? Look at the shoulders and the areas just below and on either side of the withers in the same way.

Asymmetry is not necessarily a sign that your horse is unsound. But it can be a pointer to problems, and is always worth investigating. If nothing else, you should be able to devise a work programme that will improve his musculature, which should in turn improve his way of going. If he finds his work easier, he will be less likely to resist; too many riders thinks that their horse is saying 'I won't' when in fact he is trying to tell you 'I can't'.

The horse with a good sloping shoulder is a comfortable ride and makes a saddle-fitter's job easier. Loaded shoulders make fitting much more difficult, and badly cut rugs will rub a horse in this area. A straight shoulder means the horse will naturally have an 'up and down' movement and will often tend to set himself above the bit so your choice of bit, coupled with a correct schooling programme, is important.

Different types of horse have different types of conformation. For the ultimate comparison, take the Thoroughbred and the Shire – one built for speed and the other built for power. A horse's conformation may be correct for its type, but still pose special challenges when choosing and fitting tack and equipment.

Cobs are a good example. They are the ultimate fun horses, all-rounders who can turn their hoof to anything from showing to jumping. A well-made cob is a lovely ride – but he can also present you with a few problems! Inevitably, he has a broad back and no withers, and it takes a lot of skill to fit a saddle that does not slip forwards . . . it is, after all, a bit like trying to fit a saddle on a barrel.

*Oscar is a lovely horse with a powerful jump, but is another one who poses problems for the saddle-fitter! He is particularly broad and has loaded shoulders.*

You may also have to search hard for rugs that fit well. Show cobs in particular are broad in the chest and broad in the backside, with thick necks (in comparison to lighter weight horses) and deep girths. Finding a rug that fits at the neck and chest, does not pull down over the spinous processes and can accommodate a powerful set of hindquarters – all contained in a little powerhouse of a horse that does not exceed 15.1hh – may necessitate finding a company that will make to measure.

## Head and mouth

The shape of your horse's head, its proportion to the rest of his body and the way it is set on to his neck needs to be taken into consideration when choosing bits and bridles. A horse with a proportionally big head naturally has more weight on his forehand; this often goes hand in hand with a short, thick neck, which actually makes life easier than if you have a large head on a slender neck. Again, your work regime and the tack you use will be geared to getting him off his forehand and bring his back end underneath him.

Bridles are usually made in pony, cob and full sizes, but you may need to mix parts to get a comfortable fit. For instance, a pony with a broad forehead may need a cob-size or full-size browband, whereas a Thoroughbred with a tapering muzzle may need a full-size headpiece and browband but a cob- or pony-size noseband. Missing small details can lead to big problems: a browband that pinches the ears can result in a horse that shakes its head and/or becomes difficult to bridle.

Run your fingers down each side of his head, pressing in gently and following the line of the bridle cheekpieces. If he tosses his head or moves away from your touch, it could be a sign that his teeth need attention. It is vital that every horse and pony, whether or not it is in work, has its mouth and teeth examined at least once a year by a vet who is interested in dentistry and appreciates its importance, or a specialist equine dental technician.

It is not a good idea to try poking around in your horse's mouth to check for sharp edges. Unless you have the knowledge and the use of a veterinary gag to hold the horse's mouth open, you are likely to lose a finger or two. Horses have very powerful jaws, and if they close them while your hand is inside, they can do a lot of damage without meaning to.

The horse's top jaw is wider than the bottom one, so when he chews his food only parts of his teeth become worn. The outside of the top molars and the inside of the bottom ones are not ground down, resulting in sharp edges. Put a bit in the mouth of a horse with sharp teeth and the result is pain and therefore resistance.

Watch your horse eat. If he drops bits of food out of his mouth while he is chewing, he could have teeth problems. Excess salivation is sometimes another clue that all is not well; everyone knows that a horse needs a wet mouth to lubricate the bit and be comfortable with it, but a horse who constantly chomps his bit and/or grinds his teeth is often tense and uncomfortable.

Just to make life even more complicated, mouth resistances are not always a sign that the horse is uncomfortable there. They can be an indication of tension, which may or may not be linked to pain elsewhere. However, if you eliminate mouth problems you eliminate the first and obvious cause.

Horses, like people, can have all sorts of mouth problems ranging from uneven bite to ulcers and abscesses. One of the commonest, apart form sharp molars, is wolf teeth – small, shallow-rooted vestigial molars which interfere with the action of the bit. They are easily removed without anaesthetic, and most vets and dentists do this as a matter of course.

Do not confuse wolf teeth with tushes, which are the last teeth to come through and can cause a lot of discomfort while they are doing so. Once they have erupted and settled down they rarely cause any problems, but if your four- to five-year-old suddenly starts being 'mouthy' and resistant, this could be a possible cause.

It is important to look at the shape of your horse's mouth and the shape of his tongue, because this will affect the type of bit he is comfortable with. If the bars of the mouth (where the bit rests) are short, he will often be uncomfortable with a single-jointed bit or one with a fat mouthpiece and you will need to look at alternatives.

A tongue which is thick and fleshy takes up a lot of room in the horse's mouth: add a bit with a thick mouthpiece and you immediately cause problems, because he will not be able to close his mouth properly. This in turn means that his mouth will be permanently dry rather than lubricated by saliva, which can lead to bruising.

Some horses have very long tongues, which also makes it difficult for them to close their mouths. Again, you will have to look at lighter, thinner mouthpieces – and make extra sure they are adjusted high enough in the mouth.

## On the move

The final stage of your assessment is to examine the movement of your horse or pony both in a straight line and on the lunge. He should wear only a headcollar: no lungeing cavesson, roller, saddle, side reins, protective boots or other equipment. This is because you want to see him move as naturally as possible, without the influence of any piece of tack or equipment. A lot of people may throw up their hands in horror at the idea of lungeing without protective boots, but all you are asking your horse to do is walk and trot a large circle.

The reason for using a headcollar rather than a cavesson is that a lot of horses dislike the lunge line in front of their faces. They will either back off from it or hold their heads up and their noses out, all of which gives an inaccurate picture of your horse's posture and way of going. If you fasten the lunge line to the ring at the back of the headcollar, you are using the control point he is used to from being led.

Find a straight, level area and ask someone to lead your horse while you watch. Make sure you are somewhere safe, with no access for traffic. The handler should keep the lunge line fairly loose so that the horse has complete freedom of his head and neck. This is no time for practising show ring techniques to disguise a slightly less than straight movement or a stride that is a touch unlevel!

Stand behind your horse and watch him as he walks away from you. Next watch him coming directly towards you, then from the left side and finally from the right. Is he relaxed, or tense through his neck and back? Does he hold his head and neck straight, or slightly to one side? Are his steps even? Do his knee and hock joints flex equally, or does he pick up one leg higher than its partner? Do his hips and quarters move equally on each side?

Repeat the process in trot, then on the lunge on each rein. You are trying not so much to spot soundness problems – though if any show up you can at least do something about it straight away – but to get a picture in your mind of your horse's way of going. Follow this up by watching him in the field whenever you get the chance.

If his movement changes for the worse when he is ridden, you have a problem waiting to be put right. A good horse vet, preferably one who is a competent rider, will tell you if the horse has a physical problem and may be able to identify a cause – which could be anything from sharp teeth to muscle spasm resulting from a poorly fitting saddle. After that, it is up to you.

Hopefully, your horse will be happy and free moving – within the limits of his conformation, of course. A short-legged pony with a high knee action can hardly be expected to show the long, flowing strides of a Thoroughbred with classic conformation. Even so, the rest of this book may make you think again about the equipment you use, and why.

It may even help you save money. Tack is a big investment, and you do not want it lying around gathering dust because you made a wrong buy.

# Chapter 2
## Does your Saddle Fit?

Your saddle is probably the biggest tack investment you will make. If a good leather saddle fits the horse correctly, and is well maintained and looked after, it should last for 25 years or even more – side-saddles made in the 1920s by famous names such as Champion and Wilton or Owen are still in use, because the materials and craftsmanship that went into them were of such high quality.

There are all sorts of saddles for all sorts of purposes – dressage, jumping, endurance, racing, the so-called general purpose and so on – but whatever sort you choose, it is important that it fits the horse as well as possible. The most beautifully crafted, expensive saddle in the world is no good if it is a bad fit.

The trouble is that horses were not designed to carry riders or saddles, though we are all guilty of forgetting that. As one well-known saddler and saddle-fitter puts it, the best we can do is a damage limitation exercise. In the past few years, we have become more aware of the way saddles are designed and fitted to horses; the result is that everyone from saddlers to owners and riders ought to be aware of their responsibilities, which can only be a good thing.

To prevent problems arising, it helps to understand how the horse is made. We tend to think of them as being strong and tough, especially the heavier breeds and types, and cheerfully bandy about phrases like 'up to weight.' In fact, the horse is as susceptible to back injury as we are – maybe even more so, considering what we ask him to do.

The saddle resting on your horse's back first comes into contact with his skin, which is up to a centimetre thick. This is bonded to connective tissue called fascia, and underneath that are the muscles.

The largest mass of muscle is the longissimus dorsi, which is susceptible to damage from ill-fitting saddles. So are the trapezius muscles, which are often damaged – particularly by saddles which are too narrow in the tree. The vertebrae and dorsal spinous processes (wings of bone) are underneath the longissimus dorsi. The vertebrae are much lower than most people imagine; the only part of the backbone you can actually feel are the spinous processes.

According to vets, injuries to bone structures caused by saddles are fortunately rare. Unfortunately, injuries to the skin, the fascia and the muscles are all too common. They range from bruising and muscle spasm resulting from saddles which distribute the rider's weight badly or move about too much to skin infections and girth galls that are caused by lack of care and/or poor hygiene.

A badly fitting saddle can make a horse move in a restricted way; in really bad cases it can actually make him unsound.

This chapter is concerned purely with saddles for those who ride astride. Side-saddles and their fitting are a specialist business and a totally different ballgame, which is covered in the next chapter.

## The well-fitting saddle

How do you define a well-fitting saddle? In the simplest terms, it is one which fits the profile of the horse's back, does not interfere with his movement and distributes the rider's weight over as wide an area as possible. The latest research from America shows that a ten-stone rider needs a saddle with a bearing surface of at least 140 square inches in contact with the horse for the horse to be comfortable; knee rolls do not count. Look at a selection of saddles, both old and new, and you will find many that do not meet this criteria.

The saddle must also put the rider in a position that is comfortable and correct – but the rider comes second. The horse must always be given top priority.

To a certain extent, saddle fit and design are complementary. A saddle that has a very narrow gullet and/or narrow panels will almost certainly cause problems no matter how much time and trouble is taken to fit it. Unfortunately these design faults are seen even in some modern saddles, though they now appear to be in the minority.

The reason for such design faults, which have been incorporated into some saddles for many years, is perhaps explained by the nature of the saddle manufacturing industry. Most mass-produced saddles are made by skilled workers, some of whom deserve the title of craftsmen, who neither ride nor have any contact with horses. So while the standards of construction may be tip top, the basic design may not always be of the same high standard.

Fortunately the majority of manufacturers have realised that detailed knowledge of horse anatomy and riding is essential if their products are to be successful. By bringing in consultants who have this knowledge, including vets, physiotherapists and top riders, some companies are producing saddles whose design is starting to match their construction quality.

Conscientious riders look for expert help when buying a saddle, whether new or second hand. Saddle fitting is a specialist job – but finding someone who has both the skills and the experience has been largely a matter of luck. To fit a saddle you have to evaluate a horse's conformation and movement, identify problem areas, assess a rider and find a saddle which suits both halves of the partnership. If you are a retailer, you are usually limited by the customer working within a limited budget.

It is all very well for people like me to say that a saddle must satisfy x number of criteria, but what does a retailer do when someone walks into the shop and asks for a saddle but only has, say, £200 to spend? If the retailer refuses to help because the sum seems unrealistic, the likely outcome is that the customer will buy a cheap saddle, either privately or at auction, and will either not realise or not bother that it does not fit properly. The retailer will also lose a sale – and few can afford to stay in business that way.

The obvious solution from the retailer's point of view is to find a way of supplying a cheap saddle that will enable both horse and rider to work in comfort, whether it be a second-hand or a synthetic one. But the ultimate answer that every rider must face up to is – the buck stops with you. If you own a horse, you must have the resources to be able to care for it properly, and that includes providing well-fitting tack. If you cannot afford to do that, then you have to ask yourself if you can afford to keep a horse.

Additionally you must learn to recognise what constitutes an acceptable fit and to spot problems as soon as, or even before, they arise. Life would be a lot simpler if we could buy a saddle that fitted perfectly, ride off into the sunset and never have to bother about it again. Unfortunately, that is unlikely to happen.

With conventional saddles, one which fits well today will not necessarily fit the same horse as well three months later. Horses can change shape quite dramatically, either because they gain or lose weight or because they muscle up through work and schooling. It is therefore down to you to start off with a saddle that gives you the best possible fit and to do a checking routine every month to make sure that any adjustments are made as soon as possible.

## Saddle checks

Before you put a saddle near your horse, you need to check that there are no signs of damage or wear. The most vulnerable part of a saddle is also the most important – the tree. This is the frame on which the whole thing is constructed, and if it is damaged or weak, you risk injury to the horse's back.

Damage can range from that which is undetectable to the naked eye to the obvious – from a hairline fracture to a complete break. Sometimes even an experienced saddler will not know for sure if a tree is damaged without stripping down the saddle, but there are two simple checks which should point to possible problems:

1.  Place the saddle on a flat surface, seat upwards. Put one hand on each point pocket and press hard. If there are any creaks or grinding noises, or the points 'give' noticeably under pressure, get the saddle checked by a good saddler.
2.  Now hold the saddle with the cantle pressed into your stomach and pull the pommel towards you. Again, grinding noises or creaks are warning signs. So is twisting of the saddle or creasing of the seat. (If the saddle has a spring tree, remember that it will naturally have more give than one with a rigid tree.)

*Checking to see if there are any signs of tree damage. This Thorowgood saddle is one of the latest generation of synthetics.*

The next stage in your saddle check is to look for signs that the stitching which holds the panels in place may be broken; if there are any then the panel will shift. Turn the saddle upside down to see and feel for any bumps or unevenness. If you find any ask your saddler to investigate.

Run your fingers lightly over the panels and be aware of any hollows, lumps or unevenness – which mean that the saddle needs checking and probably re-flocking. Keep your touch light: if you press too hard, you might not have the sensitivity to discover problem areas.

Place the saddle upside down on a flat surface and check that the panels are symmetrical and not too hard. If one looks larger than the other, or is obviously out of shape, or if they have been stuffed so full that they have no give, get the saddle checked before using it.

Asymmetrical panels may have been deliberately flocked that way to take a particular horse's asymmetry into account, and if this has been done by an expert it can contribute to a good fit. A new saddle straight from the manufacturers should start off with symmetrical panels.

# On the horse

So far, so good? Then it is time to actually put the saddle on the horse, without any kind of saddle cloth or numnah to start with. Be very careful how you position it; a lot of people put their saddles too far forward. As the horse moves, the top of his shoulder blade (scapula) rotates backwards up to three inches. If the saddle is too far forward, this movement will be impeded; the horse will be restricted and unhappy and will carry himself and move in a stilted fashion, which can have knock-on effects elsewhere.

Imagine what it would be like if someone fastened a leather belt around your thighs. You would be able to move, but not as freely or naturally as you should do – to compensate, you would hold and move your shoulders and pelvis in an awkward fashion that would inevitably result in aches and pains. A badly fitting saddle can put the horse in the same position.

Often we are so used to doing what we have come to look on as simple tasks that we no longer give them the care they deserve. Putting a saddle on a horse comes into this category; too many people who ought to know better cheerfully bang it down, throw the girth over the side and fasten it up without actually making sure that the saddle is in the right place and the horse is comfortable.

For some reason we are brainwashed into doing everything with our horses from the nearside, including putting on tack and rugs. The best explanation produced for this is that gentlemen always mounted from the nearside so that their swords would not cause painful interference!

Obviously this has no relevance today, so it is always a good idea to accustom horses to be led, tacked up, rugged up and even mounted from the offside. There may be times when you are in a restricted space and have to do it this way – perhaps because you need to tack up in a horsebox – and if the horse has been accustomed to it at home he is far less likely to 'throw a wobbler'.

Whatever side you are working from, hold the saddle with one hand at the pommel and the other at the cantle and gently place it farther forward than it should eventually end up. Slide it back into place so that the coat hairs lie flat underneath it; if you slide it back just slightly too far, take it off and start again. Should you push it forward, even a little, you will be going against the lie of the coat and will cause discomfort and rubs.

Go to the offside of the horse to drop the girth down; if you take advantage of a good natured animal and drop it down from the nearside, it may bang his elbow and startle him. Go back to the nearside, pick up the girth and fasten it just tight enough to keep the saddle in place, making sure it is not twisted.

Some saddles have two girth straps, while others are made with three. Three straps are preferable because they give you a temporary spare if one breaks and also allow for greater fitting choice. If the horse has a natural 'girth line' the girth will sit where it is intended to, far enough behind the elbow not to interfere but not too far back.

In this case, use the first and third girth straps. But if the horse is herring-gutted or fit and lean, and even a correctly fitted saddle tends to slip back, you may be better off using the second and third girth straps. Similarly, using the front two straps can help if the saddle has a tendency to slip forward.

Girthing-up should always be done with care. Again, it is often done without much thought – and the rider then wonders why the horse blows himself out, swings his head round and tries to bite, or both. Put a belt round your waist and jerk it up to a tight fit and you will understand how he feels.

Many so-called 'cold backed' horses – those which are believed to resent the weight and/or coldness of the saddle when it first goes on – are actually objecting to being girthed up. Fasten the girth fairly loosely and walk the horse forward in a circle for a few steps, then tighten the girth one hole.

Repeat the process until the girth is tight enough to ride but not too tight, walking him forward each time. It will only take a couple of minutes and is time well spent, especially if it leaves the horse feeling relaxed, not tensing his back or even trying to buck.

You should be able to get the flat of your fingers between the girth and the horse's side before you mount. The final stage before you do so is to stand in front of him, lift his foreleg at the knee and pull it gently forward in a straight line. This helps to ensure that the skin under the girth is smooth, not wrinkled and pinched.

It also helps to ensure his freedom of movement. If he is restricted by his girth, so will his paces be. Most horses get used to this procedure very quickly and will even offer you a front leg as you finish tightening the girth and go to stand in front of them.

The starting point of a well-fitting saddle is a tree which is the correct width and shape for the individual horse. Many saddles are made on either narrow, medium or wide fittings, with nothing in between, though some ranges are also available with 'in between' sized trees: narrow to medium and medium to wide.

If the tree is too narrow, which is the most usual mistake, it will pinch on either side of and below the withers, affecting the trapezius and triceps muscles. However, a tree that is too wide can cause just as many problems – in this case, the saddle will press on and just below the withers, again affecting the trapezius.

An experienced fitter and a good saddler (hopefully, but not necessarily, the same person) can fine tune saddle-fitting by making adjustments to the flocking. However, no amount of re-arranging flocking can compensate for a tree that is the wrong width to start with.

There are adjustable trees, but although they are hailed as the invention of the decade they have not met with very much success. They incorporate a cog, which can be turned with a special 'key' from the outside to widen or narrow the front arch; in theory they could be adjusted by any competent owner, but in practice a lot of riders found them disappointing and the demand was not as great as manufacturers expected.

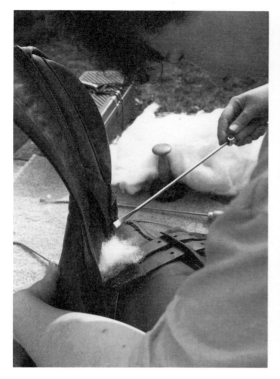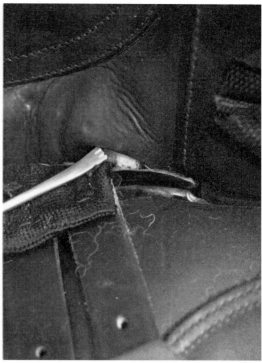

*Malan Goddard adjusts the saddle flocking to re-balance it for the individual horse. It is then pummelled in to give an even weight-bearing surface with no lumps or bumps.*

A few – very few – saddlers will bring out a selection of trees and, once they have decided on the right one, make a saddle for you from scratch. Most people have to rely on a saddler finding the right tree in the best width for their horse and making fine adjustments to the flocking.

Logic dictates that to achieve the necessary wide bearing surface, the tree must follow the contours of the horse's back. This means that for most horses of average conformation, the 'deep seated' saddle constructed on trees with a pronounced dip – rather like a banana – is totally unsuitable.

It may seem comfortable for the rider who is happy to adopt the armchair position it encourages, rather than strive for a balanced, independent seat, but it will inevitably result in uneven contact with the horse's back and too much movement. This in turn will lead to discomfort and pressure points.

Pressure points mean that eventually the blood supply to that area is restricted or even cut off. The long-term effect is muscle wastage and deep-seated damage – a horrifying prospect. The 'banana tree' can also encourage too much movement at the back of the saddle, pressure in the centre and a build-up of scar tissue at the back of the shoulder blade.

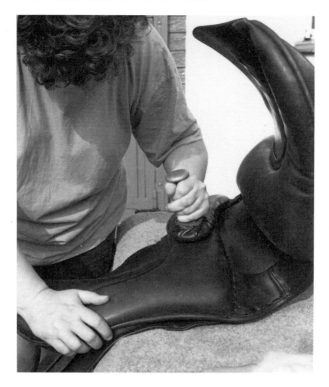

However, there is one sort of horse for whom this sort of tree is actually a godsend, namely the animal with a dipped or sway back – which can be either a natural conformation defect or one acquired through old age. Because the banana tree conforms to his profile, it provides the best fit and largest bearing surface.

When the horse is girthed up for riding, the saddle should look as if it follows the line of his back, not as if it is perched on top. When you are buying a new saddle (new as in different – the same applies to a second-hand one) an experienced fitter will soon have a shortlist of saddles which may be suitable and will make the final selection process with the rider on board.

If you are checking your existing saddle that started off as a good fit, you need either a reliable helper or a rider the same size and weight as yourself. Stand the horse square, so that he is not automatically putting himself and the saddle off balance, and either mount up yourself or put up your helper.

Whenever possible, always use a mounting block or get a leg-up rather than mounting from the ground. This applies to all riders, all horses and all circumstances! Mounting from the ground puts strain on the saddle tree, which can eventually twist it, and also puts unnecessary strain on the horse's back.

Next time you are riding in company, perhaps at a show, watch how many people heave themselves up from the ground and pull the saddle over to the left as they do so.

*This is a beautifully made synthetic saddle, but the tree is the wrong profile for this horse (the awkward four-year-old from page 9). It does not sit evenly on his back and would move about with a rider on board.*

They then settle themselves in the saddle and if they notice that the saddle is lopsided, stand in their stirrups and put as much weight as possible in the offside one to 'even things up'. Poor horse, and poor saddle.

The observer should then look at the horse, rider and saddle and check the following:

- The saddle should be level from front to back, and the rider should be balanced, neither tipped forwards nor backwards.
- Stand behind the horse to see if the saddle is sitting evenly. If it is over to one side, is it because the rider mounted from the ground or because he or she has uneven stirrup leathers and is putting more weight in one stirrup than the other?
- Still standing behind, look down the saddle gullet to see that it is clear of the horse's back all the way along, especially under the rider.

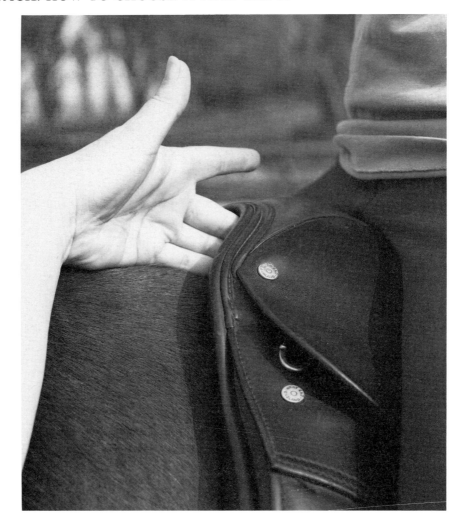

*A saddle must allow sufficient clearance at the withers. The saddle-fitter, Malan Goddard, is a rare example of someone who combines the saddlemaker's craft with a wide knowledge of horse anatomy and movement.*

- The panel should be in contact with the horse. Run your hand down the front of the panels on either side of the withers, then under the rider's thigh and behind him.
- The pommel must clear the withers and the cantle clear the back. The traditional dictate, which you may still hear quoted, is that you should be able to fit three fingers between the pommel and the horse's withers and also between the cantle and his back when a rider is on board. In practice, it may sometimes be impossible to achieve this. The amount of clearance needed often depends on the work the horse is asked to do; for instance, jumping usually requires greater clearance than hacking or dressage.

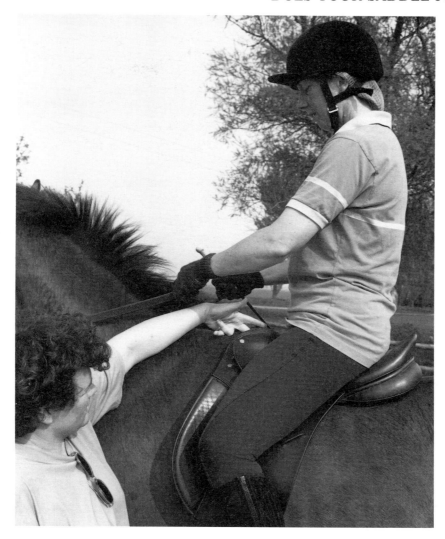

When the rider stands in the stirrups, put one finger between the pommel and the horse's withers. If it gets pinched, the saddle will come down too low.

If all is well, horse and rider can move off. As always, warm up gradually and work equally on both reins – start in walk and when you are ready, move into trot. Notice the horse's reactions and compare them to your assessment when he moved on the lunge without any restrictions.

Is he moving as freely as he did then, or does he show signs of resistance? If his stride is restricted, or if he shows any signs of tension or discomfort – which could range from swishing his tail to putting his head up and going in a hollow rather than a relaxed outline – something is wrong. Does he show the same reactions all the time, or is it only when he bends or turns?

Any saddle is bound to move slightly, but you do not want to see noticeable rocking, whether it be backwards and forwards or from side to side. Remember that you are not looking at the saddle in isolation, but at the saddle, the rider and the horse. If one side of this triangle is out of balance – a saddle that does not fit, a lame horse (for whatever reason) or an unbalanced rider – you will have a problem.

The professional saddle fitter's nightmare is the rider who insists that the saddle is at fault, when the real root of the problem is that he is unbalanced. Not surprisingly, a lot of riders take offence when it is suggested, perhaps accurately, that the problem could best be solved by a few lessons from a good instructor.

As a saddle is fitted and later adjusted for an individual horse, it stands to reason that ideally, each horse should have its own saddle. This is obviously impossible in dealers' yards, where the horses only stay for a few weeks or even less, but it is a rule that private owners should follow. With one exception, there is no such thing as a saddle that 'fits everything' – that exception is the Reactorpanel saddle (see Chapter 3) and even that can only be switched from horse to horse if they all need the same tree width and the removable panels are set up correctly.

Nor can you turn a badly fitting saddle into one that fits well by using numnahs, pads or boosters. In fact, these can often do more harm than good: put a thick numnah under a saddle that fits well without it and you are doing the equivalent of trying to wear three pairs of thick socks inside a pair of shoes that under normal circumstances are the right size for you.

If you have a particular reason for using a certain type of numnah, tell your saddler when he or she fits and makes adjustments to the saddle. Do not have a saddle fitted without a numnah and then put one underneath – unless it is a cotton numnah that is so thin it does not make any difference. Even so, be careful about using the type with thick wool pads in the withers area if you do not have a lot of leeway in that area.

## Fitting the saddle to the rider

The horse should always be the first priority when saddles are fitted, but obviously the rider must also be taken into consideration. The seat needs to be large enough to accommodate the rider's backside comfortably – but if you have a large rider on a small horse, make sure that by choosing a saddle large enough for the rider, you do not end up with one that is too long and puts pressure farther back on the horse than it should do. In this situation, the rider should either manage with a saddle that is slightly too small, or buy a horse that is the right size!

Saddle seats are measured in inches by most companies. The usual sizes are 14–18 inches in one inch increments; these cater at one end of the scale for small ponies and tiny riders, and at the other for large horses and more generously proportioned owners.

If you are a tiny rider on a large horse, you should again suit your horse first – the greater the weight bearing surface available, the better.

A small rider will find it easier and more comfortable to ride on a saddle that is too big for him than will a large rider on a saddle that is too small. Some event riders prefer seats that are theoretically too large, as it gives them that much more leeway over drop fences.

A saddle that fits the rider will help him stay in balance, encourage a correct position (and therefore an effective one: we are not talking about merely sitting pretty) and help him to stay in control. To achieve these aims, it must be the right type of saddle for the job, as is explained in Chapter 3, and suit the rider's proportions as much as possible.

For instance, if the flaps are too long, they will catch on the tops of long riding boots. If the flaps are designed so that the rider's thighs hang over them at the back, it diminishes his security and comfort.

If the knee rolls are in the correct place for you, your knee will sit just behind them when your stirrups are at the correct length for the saddle's design and function – such as when you are riding at jumping length on a jumping saddle or a forward cut general purpose saddle. Some saddles have movable knee rolls which fasten on with a special kind of Velcro.

Modern saddles inevitably have recessed stirrup bars that are fixed underneath the tree instead of on top. These are much more comfortable for the rider, as they prevent the buckles and stirrup leathers digging into the thighs.

Progress is now being made away from the saddlery trade's worst traditional legacy – the hinged stirrup bar. These were made so that the hinge on the end could be left down for riding or put up for leading the horse; the theory was that if you led a horse with the bar in the down position, the stirrup leathers and irons might slip back and fall off, though this never actually seemed to happen.

The problem with such bars is that if a rider forgot to put the hinged end down again, the leathers could not fall off if he did. If his foot did get caught (which admittedly should not happen providing the rider wore safe footwear and used stirrup irons of the correct size) the leathers could not slide off and he may be dragged. Fortunately, many modern manufacturers are starting to use open-ended stirrup bars without a hinged end.

Many riders – and manufacturers – do not realise that the siting of the stirrup bars makes a big difference to the rider's position and therefore his influence on the horse. This is particularly important with dressage saddles.

Assuming you will be aiming for the classic position, which puts you in balance with the horse, from the side, you should be able to drop an imaginary perpendicular line through the rider's shoulder, hip and heel. The widest part of your foot should rest on the stirrup iron, and if the stirrup bars are positioned correctly, the stirrup leathers will hang straight. However, if the bars are set too far forward, the rider will have to draw his leg back all the time to achieve the 'correct' position – and thus will be fighting against the saddle design.

For jumping, the leg is usually on the girth rather than just behind it, so slightly forward set bars are not a problem and may even be helpful. Some saddle manufacturers are now using adjustable stirrup bars which allow you to alter the bar's position according to the standard of the rider and the activity involved, although I have yet to meet anyone who can ride on the last adjustment without undergoing contortions!

You do not need a degree in biology to work out that male and female anatomies are different. One of the worst moments for a novice male rider is apparently when he is trying to master the rising trot and fails to synchronise his sitting and rising with the horse's stride, with painful results! But some women also have problems, especially dressage riders, and it is really no laughing matter.

Some experts say that the problem lies with the rider's position; not surprisingly, those that hold this view tend to be male trainers. But as women do not have the same shaped pelvis as men – namely wider seatbones, lower and wider pubic arches and a shorter coccyx – logic dictates that the same saddle will come into contact in a different way.

The only answer is to try different makes of saddle until you find one that fits your horse and allows you to ride in comfort. At least one firm of saddle-makers has designed a range of saddles specifically to try and solve this problem.

## Saddle-fitting and new technology

Until recently saddle-fitting has relied purely on the fitter's eye and experience. However, a new development called SaddleTech has revolutionised the possibilities and could be a vital tool for the saddle-fitters of the future.

SaddleTech was developed in America, following on from work done to prevent pressure sores in bed-ridden human patients and people who spent a lot of time in wheelchairs. For the first time, it allows those trained in its use – who must also be familiar with equine anatomy, saddles and their fitting, and riding – to see what is happening underneath the saddle.

In simple terms, a pressure-sensitive pad, which contains sensors with a force-sensitive ink, is placed under the horse's saddle. With a rider on board, the system puts a graphic display on to a computer colour monitor which shows where and how much pressure is placed on the horse's back.

The computer 'map' reveals pressure areas that are undetectable to the most skilled eye. As this book was published, there was only one SaddleTech unit in commercial use in Britain, but another was being used as part of a research project at the department of veterinary medicine at Cambridge University.

# Chapter 3
## Saddle Design

Over the past few years there have been all sorts of 'new' saddle designs coming on to the market, but basically they all fit into one of seven categories – dressage, jumping, general purpose, showing, endurance, racing and side-saddles. Specialist jobs demand different riding positions, which a saddle must allow for. To take two extremes, compare the jockey's seat, using extra-short stirrups and back almost parallel to that of the horse, with the advanced dressage rider and his deep seat, long stirrups and straighter leg.

Unfortunately, buying an expensive dressage saddle does not mean that you will automatically acquire a deep, balanced, independent seat any more than riding in a specialist jumping saddle will enable you to soar over five foot fences. If your riding is of a high enough standard, such a saddle will enhance it – but in the case of dressage saddles, the last thing you want is to be forced to ride with longer stirrups and with your legs farther back than your current state of balance allows you to cope with.

Similarly, riding a course built for a top grade showjumper is very different from negotiating an unaffiliated two foot nine showjumping class, or even one at the lower levels of affiliated competition. Under these conditions, most riders will find a general purpose saddle in which either the flatwork or jumping position predominates is perfectly adequate and even preferable.

## The GP saddle

In theory, the idea of a general purpose saddle that is all things to all riders is flawed. In practice, you should be able to find one that suits you by working out your priorities – though you may still have to compromise a little.

Ideally, each horse and rider would have two saddles, one for flatwork and one for jumping (unless, of course, you never want to jump). Unfortunately, that means spending a lot of money which many riders cannot spare.

If you want to do a lot of jumping, look for a GP saddle with a fairly forward cut. You should still be able to stay in balance when hacking out and schooling on the flat, but you will find that the knee rolls only offer support when riding with shorter stirrups.

The longest stirrup length most people are comfortable with in this sort of design is a 'long hacking' one – take your feet out of the stirrups, hold the pommel with one hand and bring your knees forward and then out to the sides, finally dropping them down into a relaxed position. This is a classic exercise which is well worth doing. It encourages you to ride with your thigh in contact and your leg long and relaxed, but not forced.

When your legs are in this position, the stirrup iron should be level somewhere between the middle of your ankle bone and an inch below it; for most people, the former is more comfortable than the latter. If your leathers are any longer, you will probably be reaching for them and in turn jeopardising your security and balance; if they are any shorter, you will tend to ride with your lower leg a bit too far forward.

Riders who want to hack out and concentrate on flatwork, perhaps competing at Preliminary and Novice dressage, should be comfortable in a straighter cut GP saddle. Take a look, too, at some of the saddles designed for working hunters; these are designed to show off the horse's shoulder and provide an established rider with adequate support for a straightforward three foot six to three foot nine course. Although they are not designed specifically for flatwork, some types are very suitable for it.

Event riders competing at Intermediate and Advanced level usually prefer dressage saddles for this phase, but GP saddles are more numerous at Pre-novice and Novice level. There are several saddles marketed as 'eventing' saddles, described – often accurately – by their makers as being suitable for both flatwork and jumping.

If you compare their designs, you will inevitably find that they could be equally described as forward cut GP saddles. Giving them the 'eventing' title is often a clever marketing ploy!

Anyone who has seen riders negotiating cross-country courses at the big events will have realised that their ability to cope with such a wide variety of fences – ranging from wide steps to huge drops – depends on a secure lower leg and a flexible upper body position. For this reason, many top riders deliberately choose saddles with flattish seats and without big knee rolls.

At first glance, they might look horrifyingly insecure. But the close contact and freedom of upper body movement they offer actually provide the skilful cross-country rider with more opportunity to remain in balance with the horse – perhaps the most vital attribute of all when it comes to staying on.

## The dressage saddle

A well-designed dressage saddle should help the rider to sit correctly, but not restrict him or her in any way. You should get the impression that the rider is sitting 'into' the horse, not perched on top of it.

As dressage is supposed to epitomise communication with the horse, the skilled rider needs to feel as much of the horse's movement as possible. This calls for close contact, and many riders (and/or saddle-makers) believe that this demands a short girth so there is as little bulk as possible under the rider's leg.

*A dressage saddle should help the rider to sit correctly, as this one does. The saddle is used with a thin cotton numnah that will not affect the fit and the numnah has been fitted so it does not press on the withers or spine.*

With tack, as in all things to do with horses, there is rarely one way of looking at things. Some newer designs now have conventional girth straps, as riders started to question whether or not the added bulk of the girth buckles actually made any difference. A saddle designed to take an ordinary girth can have three girth straps instead of the two supplied for a short one, which gives a greater range of adjustment.

A dressage saddle should have either an adjustable or an extended stirrup bar to facilitate the straighter leg position. Although the final position on an extended bar – the one farthest away from the pommel – is usually so far back that only a contortionist would be comfortable riding with his legs in that position!

## The jumping saddle

A dressage saddle will have a straight pommel, or one that slopes only slightly, to allow for the straighter panels and flaps. The pommel of a jumping saddle or a more forward cut GP model will have more slope to it, as will the panels and flaps. This is to allow for a shorter stirrup length.

Just how forward cut a saddle you choose depends on the jumping style you favour. There has been a move away from the 'monkey on a stick' jumping position, where the rider has his weight out of the saddle and is sitting forward all the time, towards a more upright one – though obviously the horse must still be given the freedom of its head and neck and the rider must fold forwards from the hips to stay in balance with and not interfere with his mount.

The reason for this shift in position may be the influence of the Continental riders, or possibly that after two extremes of riding style a more balanced approach has developed. If you look back at how riding styles have evolved, it went from the old fashioned and (thankfully) largely forgotten English hunting seat, where the rider leaned back and stuck his legs forwards 'in case the horse pecked on landing' to the style developed by Frederico Caprilli.

Caprilli, an Italian cavalry officer and instructor, saw that if riders adapted their seats to the way a horse balanced itself over a fence, rather than hampering them with a backwards seat, jumping would be easier and safer for both. With the old hunting seat, the rider's weight fell on the horse's loins, which is the most vulnerable area of the back, and he was forced to jump with a flat back and a restricted neck and head.

Caprilli's system had the rider adopt a forward seat for most of the time, from approach to landing, which allowed the horse freedom over a fence but limited the rider's influence between fences. Thanks perhaps to the Continental and American riders, who showed that the bits between the fences are just as, if not more, important than the fences themselves, most of the top showjumpers and certainly event riders adopt a more upright approach.

In some ways it is dangerous to categorise styles too much, but basically the best and most successful jumping riders are those who keep themselves and their horses balanced by adapting their position according to the demands of a course. Watch an artist like John or Michael Whitaker approaching a big vertical and you will see him sitting light but fairly upright on the approach, riding the horse forward in a rhythm but with his hocks underneath him. As the horse takes off, a rider of this calibre will keep his lower leg secure and fold forward from the hips, allowing with his hands to give the horse complete freedom of head, neck and shoulders.

The upshot of these developments are that many modern specialist showjumping saddles have a less exaggerated forward cut than their immediate predecessors, though are still cut more forward than a GP saddle.

How do you know when your GP saddle is no longer suitable for the courses you are tackling? In general, a GP saddle should be adequate for anything up to and including the lower levels of affiliated jumping, but once you were riding four-foot courses and over you would probably need to think again.

Generalisations can be misleading, of course – including that last one! That guideline carries with it the assumption that you take your horse's jumping style into account. A more forward cut saddle may give you greater security on a horse that explodes over a fence, even over a three-foot course, whereas a GP saddle may be comfortable for the rider of an economical jumper to a much higher level.

## The showing saddle

A showing saddle has to reveal a horse's conformation to the best advantage and be comfortable enough for both rider and judge – which adds up to quite a tall order. A lot of amateur exhibitors forget to take the judge into account, but if he (and in this

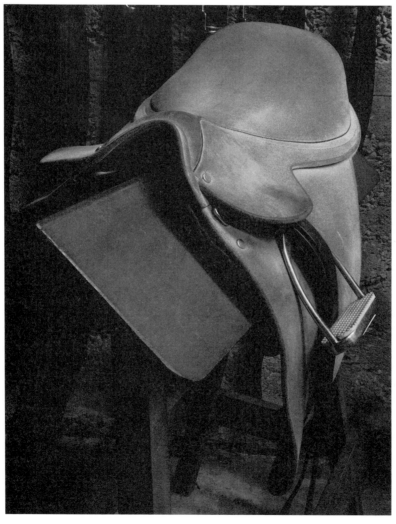

*This showing saddle is covered in reversed hide. It has a flat seat and straight flaps to show off the horse's shoulder.*

situation it usually is he) is uncomfortable on your saddle, he may assume that your horse is an uncomfortable ride and mark you down accordingly.

If you are particularly small, choose a saddle to use in the show ring that fits your horse but is a bit big for you. This is important if you are showing in hunter or cob classes, because a substantial horse looks downright silly with a tiny saddle. You are aiming to give an impression of harmony – admittedly a tiny rider who looks like a pea on a drum might detract from that, but there is not a lot you can do about it!

Judges of hunters and cob classes are often on the well-built side, as they tend to specialise in the sort of horses they would buy for themselves. A small rider can cope quite easily with a saddle that is too big, but a large rider will be uncomfortable (or worse!) on a saddle that is too small.

Showing judges look for a horse with a sloping shoulder, which makes for athleticism and good paces. Your saddle should therefore show off the shoulder, not cover it up.

When the horse is tacked up, the saddle needs to look as if it follows the lines of his back – not as if it 'cuts him in two'. For this reason, choose one with a flattish seat.

Professional showing riders prefer suede saddles both for appearance and the extra bit of security they give. Old saddles of this type by legendary manufacturers such as Owen are much sought after; the quality of the materials and workmanship was so high that they go on forever, albeit with regular checks and occasional maintenance.

Some riders, particularly those in hack classes, use dressage saddles. Often the straight cut of these is too severe and the eye is drawn to the buckles of the short girth. As you want the judge to look at the horse, not its tack, this defeats the object.

For a detailed look at tack for showing, see *Showing to Win* by Carolyn Henderson and Lynn Russell, published by Swan Hill Press.

## Endurance saddles

Endurance horses and ponies wear tack and carry riders for much longer than those in other disciplines, over all sorts of terrain and at varying speeds. This means that the saddle (and the bridle) must fit both horse and rider superbly and be kept in top condition.

It must also allow the rider to adjust his length of stirrups and still remain in balance. This is not only for the sake of the horse – so the rider can ride in half seat for some of the time and re-distribute his weight – but to aid the rider's own comfort. If your leg muscles start to protest, lengthening or shortening your stirrups by even a hole can make a lot of difference.

The best endurance saddles are designed to give the widest possible weight distribution, which of course should be a prerequisite of every saddle. They are usually cut fairly straight, as endurance riders are not officially required to jump. They must be as stable as possible; when you are going up and down steep hills, the last thing you want is a saddle that slips forwards or backwards.

*An endurance saddle designed to be comfortable for horse and rider over long distances. It is fitted with English stirrup irons.*

Endurance riders tend to lead the way forwards in every aspect of horse care. Much research has gone into and is being put into designing the ideal endurance saddle; innovations of the past few years include the Ortho-Flex saddle, which originated in America.

This has panels that bolt on to the tree and can be adjusted to each individual horse. A possible drawback is that it takes a skilled eye to fine tune the adjustments. The saddle is also expensive enough to put it out of many riders' reach.

The Reactorpanel saddle (see later in this chapter) should also find a welcome in the endurance world. As with all new ideas, the basic design has been constantly refined as riders with different types of horse in different disciplines test it at full stretch.

## Side-saddles

Side-saddle riding has enjoyed a boom in popularity in recent years. Once dismissed as old fashioned and restricting, it has attracted a new generation of devotees who find its elegance captivating and appreciate the security it gives. Experts say that it is easier to acquire a secure, balanced seat when riding side-saddle than it is when riding astride – and some riders who had to give up conventional riding because of back or hip problems find that switching to side-saddle allows them to ride in comfort once more.

Experts who can make and fit side-saddles are now few and far between. This means that old side-saddles by legendary makers – such as Owen, Champion and Wilton, Mayhew and Whippy – are much sought after, even if they need restoring. As with some of the old showing saddles, the quality of the materials and the workmanship was so high that they could well outlast some modern saddles.

Most side-saddles weigh about two stones. Traditionally, they were custom-made for individual clients, and saddlers would take a wide range of body measurements. They

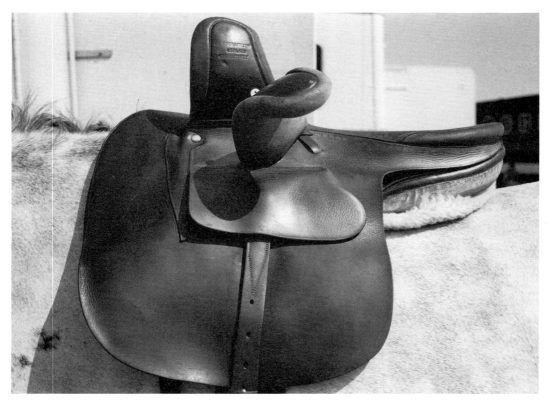

*Side-saddles have special girthing arrangements to keep them in place. Their fitting is a specialist job and there are very few people who are expert in it.*

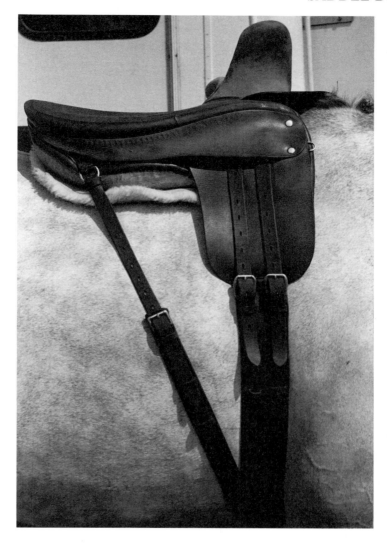

were also made so that ladies who rode daily could ride on the nearside and on the offside; it was believed that this helped to prevent curvature of the spine, but it probably did more for the horses' backs than that of the riders.

Side-saddles and those made for riding astride have very different basic constructions. The tree of an ordinary saddle fits across the withers and is adjusted equally on either side, but a side-saddle tree is longer on the nearside than the offside.

This means that you start off with an imbalance; add two pommels on the nearside and none on the offside and you upset the balance even farther! This is where the skills of the saddle-fitter and the saddler come in; a specialist can do a lot with clever flocking, but you do need a specialist. It is very unlikely that a saddler who has only had experience of ordinary saddles, no matter how good they are, can cater for a side-saddle rider.

The two pommels on a side-saddle are called the fixed head and the leaping head. The fixed head is the top one, and supports the rider's right leg, whilst the lower leaping head is a support for the left thigh. The seat is flat, unlike that of an astride saddle, and is often covered in suede for extra security.

Side-saddles usually have three straps as part of the girthing arrangement: an ordinary girth, a balance strap and a safety strap or surcingle. The balance strap is designed to keep the weight of the saddle equal on the horse's back, and some animals are worried about it when the side-saddle is first put on.

It is sensible to fasten the balance girth just tight enough to keep things in place and to lead the horse forward. Walk him round until he gets used to the feel of it, and tighten it gradually. Make sure the saddle is not put on so that the balance strap is too far back and/or too tight. If this happens, it turns into a bucking strap – and most horses will react accordingly!

It is vital that your side-saddle has a safety fitting so that the stirrup leather can be released in an emergency. As an extra safety measure, never ride side-saddle on a horse who is known to rear – if he goes over backwards, the only way the rider is likely to fall is underneath him.

The best way to find out about buying and fitting side-saddles – and anything else to do with side-saddle riding – is to contact the Side-Saddle Association at Highbury House, High Street, Wellford, Northampton NN6 7HT (address at time of publication). It keeps a register of instructors and a list of saddlers and second-hand side-saddles are often sold from one member to another.

## Racing saddles

Racing saddles are such a specialist market that they have only curiosity value for most riders. Many of us, when confronted by something weighing less than 1lb, cannot imagine what it is like – or even how it is possible – to ride on something so tiny and apparently so unforgiving.

The answer is that the design of the saddle complements the jockey's position, which to non-race riders looks as if it relies more on luck than logic for security. Race riding demands perfect balance; the saddle is neither needed for nor intended to give support.

Racing saddles are usually made on half trees as opposed to the full trees used for other models. New technology has resulted in synthetic saddles made on plastic trees to keep the already light weight to a minimum, but a damaged tree can still result in a horse with a damaged back.

# The Reactorpanel saddle

The Reactorpanel saddle is an exciting development in saddlery. It is the result of 26 years' research by saddler and horseman Barry Richardson, who has spent his working life trying to make the ultimate – a saddle which gives optimum weight distribution.

Barry's work with sophisticated pressure testing equipment convinced him that no matter how carefully a traditional saddle was made and fitted, it could not give him the results he wanted. He decided the only way was to start from scratch with a new approach.

His basic aim was to give the widest possible area of weight distribution. The panels had to have their own integrity and be an effective weight-bearing surface, which required a stiff layer inside that could still flex according to the way the horse moved.

After testing several types of high-tech material, Barry and his son, Phillip – a former restorer of vintage vehicle instruments – settled on a special type of plastic. This still left the problem of flexibility, but Phillip solved it by following the design principles of a cardboard baseball cap.

These caps, often given away as advertising and marketing gimmicks, are cut on a spiral to provide a fit that adapts to any wearer. This idea was adapted for the saddles, and the patented system achieved the right results; the material has been bench tested to do two million flexions without breaking.

The panels are secured to the saddle with aviation Velcro, which is very different from the ordinary kind used on brushing boots and other equipment. They are fixed on to and balanced, according to the individual horse and rider, with blocks incorporating Sorbethane, a material with great shock absorbing qualities that is also used in ejector seats.

The panels move with the horse, so are continually adjusting and re-forming. Interchangeable blocks of slightly differing sizes are supplied so that alterations can be made between one horse and another if necessary.

Re-flocking has become a thing of the past with these saddles. If the horse changes shape as he gains or loses weight, or his muscles build up through work, the panels adapt to him. It means that as long as the tree is the correct fitting, the saddle can be swapped from one horse to another and will adapt to each animal.

Although intended as a way forwards and not just as a remedial saddle, the Reactorpanel has been helpful in cases of back and gait problems. Some owners who have investigated it as a last resort have found that it has worked where nothing else seemed to.

Other owners using these saddles, including police forces, report that horses wear their shoes in a much more even way, especially on the hind feet. This is taken as an indicator of gait improvement.

The original version of this saddle incorporated top quality materials and had a price to match, but as this book was published the company behind it, Roe, Richardson, Francis and Drew, was investigating whether it could offer a budget version. It is also possible to convert many conventional saddles by replacing the original panels with Reactorpanels.

The deciding factor in whether or not a conversion is possible is the saddle tree, so each saddle has to be looked at individually. If a saddle is converted, the owner can still have it returned to its original format if desired.

The Reactorpanel saddle, which is available in different models, looks different from ordinary saddles – but most people find its appearance perfectly acceptable. If a special two-part numnah is used over the panels, the saddle looks hardly different from an ordinary one.

## Synthetic saddles

When synthetic saddles first appeared on the market they looked – and in many cases were – cheap and nasty. Modern versions are very different, and though they will never replace leather saddles, synthetics have found a definite role.

They are usually cheaper than leather saddles, which makes them an attractive proposition for many riders and retailers. They are also lightweight, easy to look after and hard wearing; a synthetic saddle will probably not last as long as a leather one that has been well looked after – or if it does, will not look as good.

Some riders like to have a synthetic saddle for everyday use, especially in bad weather, so that they can keept their leather one for 'best'. Others find that the lower prices mean that they can afford two saddles instead of one, so can have, say, a GP saddle and a dressage model.

The advantages of synthetics have been well advertised by the manufacturers. The disadvantages are that although designs have been vastly improved, some still suffer from early problems such as narrow gullets and insufficient bearing surfaces. Some tree profiles also tend to be too curved to give a good bearing surface in the finished saddle, unless the horse has the sort of dipped back conformation this profile suits.

Some riders mistakenly think that because a saddle is lightweight, it cannot do any damage. Unfortunately a poorly fitting synthetic saddle can cause just as many problems as a poorly fitting leather one. Synthetics must be fitted and maintained with the same care and expertise as traditional saddles.

The leading manufacturers of synthetic saddles – in particular Wintec and Thorowgood – must be praised for their willingness to introduce new and innovative ideas. Wintec, a company formed by the Bates brothers in Australia, has devised a system of switchable 'tops' for its saddles so that if one becomes worn, or you want to substitute a 'leather' top for a 'suede' one, you can have a new looking saddle in seconds. Kent and Masters, an associate company of Thorowgood, has done a lot of work on high-tech materials for trees and incorporates a special shock absorbing gel in its Teqnic saddle seats.

# Chapter 4
## Saddle Fittings

Your choice of saddle fittings – girth, stirrup leathers, irons and possibly some sort of numnah or pad – is as important as that of the saddle itself. So too is the way they are fitted; a girth that pinches or rubs, or a numnah which presses on the withers or alters the fit of the saddle can do more harm than many riders realise.

Because they are relatively cheap compared to a saddle, fittings are not always given high priority. But if you think about it, your life could depend on them: the most luxurious saddle in the world will not help you if the stitching on your girth gives way, or a stirrup leather breaks whilst you are galloping or jumping!

Always try to buy the best fittings you can afford and keep them in good condition and repair. (See Chapter 12 for guidelines on checking your tack for safety.) Never be tempted to say 'It's starting to wear but it will do for everyday' because your tack has to take just as much strain schooling and out hacking as it does at a show.

### Girths

Girths are made from leather or from a variety of synthetic materials. Leather is the traditional choice, especially for the show ring, and as long as it is kept clean, soft and supple looks very smart. Problems arise when it is allowed to dry out, as it becomes hard and can cause rubs and girth galls.

Do not use a leather girth, no matter how well maintained, on a horse in 'soft' condition, or one who has not worn one for some time. The traditional way of toughening up the skin was to apply surgical spirit to the girth area (provided, of course, there was no existing irritation or injury). Salt water is said to have a similar effect. If you try this, make sure the coat and skin are clean and dry before you use any girth, or you could trap residues of salt between the two.

There are two schools of thought as to whether leather or synthetic girths are most comfortable for the horse. Those who opt for leather say that 'skin on skin' is the best recipe for comfort, while synthetics fans say that anything which absorbs sweat must be better.

Whatever you choose must be used and adjusted carefully. The textbook method of girthing up is to fasten the girth to the offside, pass it under the horse's belly and adjust it on the nearside. In practice, making adjustments on both sides means that you are not expecting the same holes on the girth straps to take the strain all the time.

*Three girths in common use. The padded leather girth in the centre has elasticated ends, while the others are two types of synthetic girth.*

Always girth up carefully, following the guidelines in Chapter 2. If your horse associates being tacked up and ridden with discomfort, he will be tense and resistant before you even get on him – which does not bode well for when you ride him. Ideally, a girth should give an even pressure all the way round, but in practice this is hard to achieve.

Many horses will flinch, lay their ears back or show other signs of discomfort when handled in the girth area. Some have tell-tale white hairs, signs of old girth injuries. Even the best standard girths often give uneven pressure; one of the best designs is a humane girth developed by Barry Richardson, inventor of the Reactorpanel saddle, which was in prototype as this book was published. It incorporates enough stretch throughout the whole of its length to keep the horse comfortable, whilst the soft neoprene outer avoids the risk of rubbing.

A horse who works hard will sweat under this girth, but as long as the area is kept clean (preferably by washing or sponging off after use, as should be done in any case) it does not appear to cause any problems. The girth might look less attractive than other types off the horse, but few people would complain about its appearance when in place.

Girths with elastic inserts at *both* ends are presumably more comfortable for a hard-breathing horse. Unfortunately most manufacturers put an insert in one end only, which is more likely to give lopsided pressure. If you use one of these, it is more sensible to put the elastic end on the opposite side to the one which you intend to make most adjustments on. It would be even more sensible to replace the girth with one that has elastic inserts at both ends.

For instance, if you follow the traditional method of fastening the girth to the offside straps before you tack up and adjusting it on the nearside, put the elastic end on the offside. The reason for this is that you are less likely to pull the girth too tight without realising it. A lot of riders, particularly men, are not aware of their own strength and girth up far too tightly 'so the saddle won't slip'. If the girth is elasticated at one end and the rider hoists this up, it creates a lot of pressure at the other, which does not have any give.

Remember you should be able to slip your fingers between the girth and the horse's side before you get on – also remembering that you need to check the girth after a few minutes in case the horse blew himself out to minimise anticipated discomfort! Furthermore, it is essential to pull the horse's front legs gently forward before you are ready to mount, to reduce the risk of folds of skin getting caught up or pinched.

Synthetic girths are often not shaped, the manufacturers relying on their absorbent properties to prevent the risk of galling, but leather ones comes in various styles. The Atherstone girth is shaped in the section designed to fit behind the elbow, so the horse is less likely to suffer girth galls. (The skin behind the elbow is thinner than in many other areas, and therefore more prone to rubbing and bruising.)

The Balding girth is designed with the same aim in mind and has crossed leather pieces resembling a type of plait to keep it away from the elbow. The three-fold leather girth, once in universal use and now less common – perhaps because it is expensive – has a strip of material inside that should be kept soaked in leather food or another appropriate product to keep the leather soft and supple. This type of girth should always be put on with the rounded edge nearest to the horse's elbow, so the skin does not get pinched.

Synthetic girths can be made from various materials. The most common, and also the best, are the modern ones with a strong but absorbent outer and padding in the middle. These are often referred to as 'Cottage Craft girths' because of one of the best-known manufacturers.

The old-fashioned nylon 'string' and webbing girths are not seen very often – which is perhaps just as well! The former trapped dirt, skin and hair and acted as an invitation to girth galls, whilst webbing has a tendency to break without warning – which is why they are designed to be used in pairs.

## Stirrup leathers and irons

Stirrup leathers are made from different kinds of leather in different lengths to suit adults or children. You can also buy synthetic 'leathers', which are often strong but lack the aesthetic appeal. Some such leathers also tend to stretch round the holes and to be slightly abrasive against the flaps if used on a leather saddle.

There are various types of 'proper' stirrup leathers, all of which have advantages and disadvantages. The finest quality are oak bark, which are more difficult to obtain than they used to be because fewer firms use the lengthy oak bark tannage process. (See Chapter 12 for more information on different types of leather.)

Leathercare expert Robin Coleman says that if he was asked to pick the finest quality material for stirrup leathers, his first step would be to select hide from an aged bull: this would have a good thickness to start with. He would then expect it to go through a lengthy tanning process, so the end result would be strong leather with a tight grain.

Red chrome buffalo hide stretches, but there is resistance against breakage. Rawhide – which is cow hide as opposed to buffalo – will also stretch, but again is very strong. Rawhide is tanned from the top and back, leaving a strip of 'raw material' in the centre.

If you wanted to grade leathers in terms of sheer strength, the order would be buffalo hide, rawhide and English oak bark leather. But there are so many other factors to take into consideration that it comes down to individual preference. For instance, buffalo hide has a feel to it that some people find unpleasant, while rawhide is not as thick as it used to be. Farmers are no longer prepared to let cows live as long as they used to, purely because they do not consider it economical – and as we all know, the older you get, the thicker the hide you develop!

Most riders put more weight on one stirrup than the other, even if they do not realise it. If you use stirrup leathers that are likely to stretch, it is a good idea to swap them round every time you ride to try and keep them even. At least one company has introduced leathers with a nylon strip through the centre, rather like a leather sandwich with a nylon filling: these are strong and do not stretch, giving the best of both worlds.

Mounting from the ground is one of the easiest ways to stretch your stirrup leathers, and yet another good reason not to do it unless absolutely necessary. If you are likely to be in a situation where it is unavoidable – perhaps on long ride or out hunting, where you have to dismount for a time and no mounting block is available – it can be worth buying an extending stirrup leather.

This comprises a stirrup leather with a length of strong webbing and a hook and slot fastening at one end. The idea is that you release the hook and slot, thus lowering the leather by about six inches, to mount and then hook it up again when you are in the saddle.

For safety's sake, always run the stirrup irons up the leathers when you are leading a horse. Tuck the leathers under the bottom edge of the iron to stop them flapping about.

If you are lungeing a horse with a saddle on, either remove the stirrup irons and leathers altogether or wrap them once round the iron, then pass the loose end of the leather through the loop and through the keeper on the saddle flap to prevent the irons slipping down, banging against the horse's sides and annoying or frightening him.

Long reining a horse with his tack on is an excellent way of accustoming him to tack and 'making his mouth'. Some people long rein with a roller, while others prefer to use the saddle that the horse will wear when he is ridden. Using a saddle is a logical progression, but it is important to make sure that the long reins are held out of the way and to minimise the risk of them slipping down round his back legs.

The best way to do this is to adjust the stirrup leathers so they are shorter than normal riding length and to pass the long reins through them. Fastening the irons to the girth with a thin strap such as a spur strap will stop them banging about.

Passing the long reins through the irons restricts the degree by which you can open the reins, so many trainers prefer not to do this when they are lungeing with two reins on a circle. As they will be working the horse in a confined space, it is safe to do so – or at least, as safe as working a young/exuberant/awkward horse can ever be! But for long reining on roads and tracks, where you are working in straight lines and gentle curves, it is far safer to put the long reins through the stirrup irons or roller rings.

## Stirrup irons

It is most important that a stirrup irons should be safe. This means that they must be made from stainless steel, be the right size for the rider's foot and be heavy enough.

Stirrup irons, like bits, used to be made from nickel. There are still some around, and they belong only in the dustbin. Nickel bends and can even break, so if your horse falls and lands trapping your leg, the iron could bend and trap your foot.

Plated metal irons can be similarly light and weak. Stainless steel has a clean, bluish look to it and irons made from it will feel and look heavy and substantial.

Look at how the irons are made, too. The eye at the top of the iron, which takes the stirrup leather, should be smooth and well finished: rough edges will damage and weaken the leather. The iron itself should look smooth, free from the 'joins' that can signify plated metal.

Too many riders use stirrup irons that are too small. When the widest part of your foot rests on the tread, there should be half an inch clearance on either side. Any less means you risk your foot getting stuck, while if the iron is too large there is a danger of your foot slipping through and jamming.

Stirrup irons should be heavy enough to fall away from your foot if you fall off the horse. Such irons also hang better. Racing irons, designed to be extra lightweight, are the exception to this rule.

Safe stirrups irons can only do their job if the rider's footwear is equally safe. Properly designed riding boots are the best; *never* wear ordinary trainers or flat shoes. There are lots of fashion riding boots on the market which have been designed for casual wear, and which are both comfortable and stylish. Check before you buy them whether they are designed to be safe for riding or simply as yard boots; a good retailer, preferably one who is a member of the British Equestrian Trade Association, should be able to advise you.

If you have riding trainers with laces, fasten them in a double bow so there is no risk of them coming undone. Parents who are reluctant to buy proper boots before they know whether or not their children will enjoy riding, may want them to wear wellingtons for the first few lessons, but styles vary and they must ask the instructor's advice. Any footwear used for riding should have a defined (but never high) heel and should not have heavily ridged soles. Sandals are also unsuitable.

Riders with small feet who compete in showing classes should remember that the judge's boots may be rather larger. A judge will not be amused if he is asked to try and cram his size elevens into a pair of irons designed for your size fours. In some cases, using a pair of irons that is slightly large (but not so large that they are dangerous) will solve the problem. Alternatively, your assistant should be equipped with a spare pair of larger irons and leathers – the latter may need to be longer than the ones you use – and should make a swift changeover before the ride part of the judging.

If you thought stirrup irons were just something to put your foot in, think again. There are several designs, some aimed at giving you extra safety in the saddle.

The commonest types are the Fillis and the English hunting irons. Fillis irons have rounded sides, whereas the sides of English hunting ones are flat where they join the tread. The theory is that the flattened sides help keep the rider's foot straight, but this is debatable.

Less common designs include one aimed at cross-country riders. This has a larger than normal, oval tread supposed to give a broader base of support when the rider lands over drop fences, or the horse 'throws a big one' to get himself out of trouble.

Dressage riders sometimes opt for stirrup irons or treads supposed to encourage a correct position. These range from sloping treads to bent back heads; while they may undoubtedly help some riders, they can positively hinder others. If your natural 'conformation' means that you stand, walk and ride with, for instance, your toes slightly out, trying to force them into an unnatural position can be uncomfortable and eventually painful – and could even lead to pulled muscles.

*Fillis irons fitted with rubber stirrup treads. Compare their shape with the English irons on page 37. This handmade Reactorpanel saddle is made from top quality Austrian leather that has been textured on the seat and knee grips to provide extra security for the rider.*

We may all aim to follow classical principles of riding, but we are not all shaped to do so. If you really find it difficult to let your weight down into your heels or to adopt a correct lower leg position, invest in some lessons – perhaps on the lunge – with a good, sympathetic instructor before you buy special stirrup irons.

In theory, safety irons should be unnecessary because on a well-designed saddle the leathers and irons will slip backwards off the stirrup bars in the event of a fall. In practice, some stirrup bars are badly designed and/or set on, and the stirrups stay in

*Safety irons are an extra precaution for young riders. The rubber ring, which comes loose in the event of a fall and prevents the risk of the rider being dragged, must be on the outside edge. If hinged stirrup bars are always left down, the stirrup leathers should pull off the saddle if the rider falls – but these irons are a good back-up.*

place. Again, even if this happens, you should not be in danger providing your stirrup irons are the correct weight and size and you have safe footwear.

But for anyone who wants to take every precaution, there are special safety irons available. The commonest is the Peacock safety iron, which has a thick rubber loop to replace one side of an otherwise conventional iron. These irons *must* be used so that the elastic side is on the outside. If they are put on the wrong way round, their safety value will be lost.

If Peacock irons are used, the rubber rings must be inspected regularly and replaced when necessary. Anyone who uses this design, even children, should avoid mounting from the ground whenever possible, as the tread can become bent. This is unavoidable, as it only has support on the inside.

Simplex irons, which originated in Australia, are in many ways better than the Peacock ones. The outside 'leg' bends forwards, which is supposed to allow the foot to slip out more easily in the event of a fall. They feel different from ordinary irons, so you have to ride in them a few times to get used to them.

Racing and side-saddle irons are very specialist markets. The two main types of racing irons are exercise and actual race irons; both are made from aluminium, which cuts down on weight but is not as strong as stainless steel.

Exercise irons look like flimsier versions of Fillis irons. As the name suggests, they are used for everyday work. Racing irons are made to a 'cradle pattern' that is more comfortable for jockeys wearing thin, lightweight, boots.

Side-saddle riders can at least economise on stirrup irons – they only need one! These have a larger eye than ordinary stirrups and the outside 'leg' is bent out slightly to allow the foot to slip away more easily. There is also a side-saddle safety iron which breaks open if tipped up by a rider's fall.

Most riders these days like to use rubber stirrup treads for extra security and comfort. These can be the straightforward variety or the various angled designs mentioned earlier, which are aimed at improving a faulty leg position.

Stirrup 'shoes', which look like the front half of a shoe and fasten on to the irons, are popular with some endurance riders. The idea is that they keep the correct part of the foot on the stirrup iron and prevent it slipping too far forward; some endurance riders find it gives them extra balance and security when riding over difficult terrain. It also

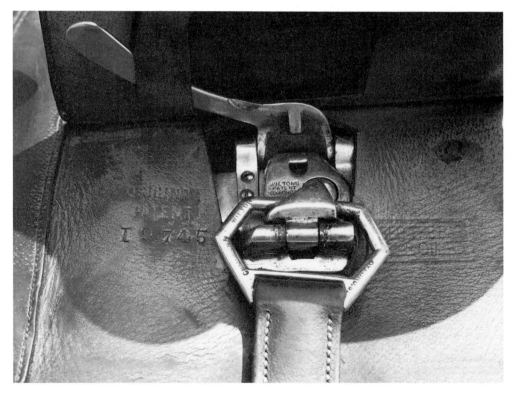

*Side-saddles should always have special safety fittings so the rider will not get trapped if she falls.*

means that if they get tired or their muscles start to protest, which can happen to even the fittest rider on a particularly tough ride, they are less likely to unbalance their horses.

These accessories are also useful for riding schools or trekking stables who are likely to attract inexperienced, would-be riders. They are an extra safety precaution which helps prevent feet clad in less than ideal footwear from slipping too far through the iron.

*A curiosity from the tackroom of showing expert and side-saddle specialist Lynn Russell. This is a groom's stirrup, carried by a groom and used so he could ride a lady's horse astride when she changed horses out hunting and sent the first one home with him.*

# Numnahs

Most riders use some form of numnah, saddle cloth or pad. Yet if you asked them why, they would probably be surprised: their use has become so universal that few people look at the reasoning behind it. The major exception is the show rider; most do not like to use a numnah in the ring because they feel it detracts from the overall picture.

Riders who have thought about why they use something under their saddle usually have three reasons. One is that they think it is more comfortable for the horse because it provides extra cushioning/shock absorption. The second is that they feel it absorbs sweat and the third is simply that is keeps the underneath of the saddle clean.

Research seems to show that, in most cases, the only one of these explanations that really holds water is the third one. Many people, including manufacturers of specialised saddle pads, will argue with that statement – but a lot of experienced saddle-fitters will agree. The reason is that if a saddle fits correctly, anything other than a thin cotton numnah or saddle cloth could adversely affect the fit; after all, if you have a pair of well-fitting shoes and wear a pair of extra thick socks, they can become tight and uncomfortable.

The same applies to saddles and numnahs. Some pads in particular can 'reduce' the width of a saddle tree by as much as half an inch, which is an awful lot. It all comes back to the same premise: if the saddle is well designed and fits your horse, he should be comfortable. If you are too heavy for him, or roll about so much that you cause problems, the answer lies with a good instructor, not a new numnah. No numnah can compensate for incorrect riding or an incorrectly fitted saddle.

A thin cotton numnah may absorb some of the horse's sweat, but it must be washed regularly if there is to be no risk of skin infection. In any case, sweat marks should always be rinsed off – with lukewarm water if necessary on a cold day, followed by appropriate rugging. Also some people argue that skin against skin is better than fabric against skin.

Unfortunately the thought that now goes into a lot of saddle design has not carried over to most numnahs. Your saddle may be designed and fitted so there is no pressure on the horse's withers or along his spine but if your numnah pulls down flat, as so many do, you can still get pressure problems. The textbook advice for using a numnah is to make sure it is pulled up into the gullet of the saddle all the way along, and while this is good advice, a lot of numnahs soon work their way out of that position.

There are two main reasons for this. One is that many numnahs which offend in this way are cut in a one dimensional way – a horse is, of course, three dimensional. The other is that the retaining loops which are designed to fix to the girth straps are set too far forward and thus drag the numnah down on the horse's back.

Some companies now offer moulded 'numnah lifters' which fit between the horse and the numnah. These are shaped to keep it up off the horse's back and withers, which in theory is a good idea. In practice, you are often simply adding another layer, which you do not need, to cope with a problem that could be eliminated by not using a numnah!

An added irritation with numnah design is that many manufacturers insist on putting bulky sheepskin-type pads, ostensibly for 'protection', in the withers area. All these do are to add unwanted bulk under the front of the saddle.

As horses and riders are all individuals, there may be occasions when a specific product can be useful for a specific partnership. But if you think your horse has a problem, you will be far better spending your money consulting your vet – perhaps in conjunction with a physiotherapist who will work to his referral – and/or saddle-fitter than on buying a 'magic saddle pad'.

Gel pads are one of the most controversial cases in point. When these first appeared on the market, they were hailed as the ultimate invention – fabric covered pads containing special shock absorbing gel were seen as a way of improving the horse's comfort as he performed athletic feats such as landing over big fences. They undoubtedly do have their uses, but they are perhaps not the universal panacea we at first hoped for.

Research using sophisticated pressure testing equipment has shown that using a gel pad may often seem to disperse unwanted pressure. But after the horse has been ridden for a while, all that happens in some cases is that the pressure points shift: while you get rid of one problem, you have to contend with another.

One of the more unusual ideas to come on to the market was a numnah incorporating small wooden balls. This was said to have a massaging effect on the horse's back, rather like the devices made to fit on car seats. However, it does not seem to be readily available now.

American riders make great use out of 'lifters' or 'risers', shaped pads designed to tip the saddle up at the front or the back. The basic argument against these is that if the saddle fits properly to start with there is no need for them.

## Seat savers

Seat savers are really numnahs for riders and perhaps have more value than numnahs for horses! The basic styles are designed simply to provide extra cushioning on the seat, thus adding to the rider's comfort and reducing the risk of saddle sores. They also protect the pommel, cantle and seat.

This makes them very useful for riders who keep their horses on livery yards and their tack at home and have to carry saddles in cars all the time. Also, some outdoor and riding jackets have heavy duty zips which can catch on or dig into the pommel, causing scratches or nicks. Again, a seat saver can help prevent this.

There are two designs available which offer added benefits. One is the Seeta, which is not so much a seat saver as a 'saddle converter', and the other is a seat saver that incorporates shock absorbing Sorbethane, which is said to help people with back problems ride more comfortably.

The Seeta, designed, made and patented by instructor Sally Evans, is a simulated sheepskin saddle cover with adjustable padding. It fits over the top of a general purpose saddle and 'converts' it to one offering more of a dressage position.

Unfortunately the British Horse Society dressage group rules prohibit the use of saddle covers in competition, but the Seeta is still useful for schooling at home. It could also help you decide whether spending money on a dressage saddle would be worthwhile.

Would-be dressage riders are not the only ones to benefit from Sally's innovation. The Seeta has been used successfully by several Riding for the Disabled groups, where the security and stability it offers have made it a useful aid for many disabled riders.

## Breastplates and breastgirths

Breastplates and breastgirths, like numnahs and saddle pads, should never be used to compensate for a badly fitting saddle. However, they may be needed on a horse who has a powerful front but is either slab-sided or herring-gutted – so that even with the attentions of a good saddle fitter, his saddle has a tendency to slip back.

They also offer extra security if you are riding up and down steep hills or jumping substantial drop fences. Event riders often regard them as vital safeguards, together with an overgirth (which will hopefully hold the saddle in place should the ordinary girth break – it has been known!).

A breastplate looks rather like half a martingale; it fastens to the girth and then goes between the front legs before dividing into a neckstrap with small metal rings either side of the withers. Connecting straps go from these rings to the D-rings at the front of the saddle.

Breastplates usually come with detachable martingale fittings. Make sure they are adjustable, or you will often not be able to get the correct fit. Do not adjust a breastplate so tight that it restricts the horse when galloping or jumping.

Breastgirths are often used on hurdlers and National Hunt horses as a precaution to stop their lightweight saddles slipping back as they jump. They can also, of course, be used in other spheres; some people prefer breastplates, others breastgirths.

The difficulty with fitting a breastgirth is that it must be tight enough to do its job, but not so tight that there is a danger of it pressing on the horse's windpipe. Striking a balance between the two is easier said than done, but you should be able to get a hand's width between the front of a leather breastgirth and the horse. Breastgirths with elasticated fronts allow more leeway in adjustment.

*A breastplate, modelled by Pewter – one of the residents at the International League for the Protection of Horses' headquarters in Norfolk. Pewter's loose ring Fulmer snaffle is usually worn with leather keepers which attach the top of the bit cheeks to the bridle cheekpieces.*

*This horse has rather more tack than is usually seen on one animal! He wears a double bridle with a Flash noseband and sheepskin sleeve, a breastgirth and breastplate with running martingale attachment – and under the saddle, a sheepskin numnah and a gel pad.*

*Cruppers are sometimes seen on ponies and are used in an attempt to stop the saddle slipping forwards. They are not a substitute for a correctly fitting saddle. The numnah used under this pony's saddle is so thick that it could affect the fit.*

# Chapter 5
## Bitting

Bits and bitting can cause more controversy and confusion than any other subject in the horse world. You can guarantee that in any group of people you will find areas on which they disagree, no matter how knowledgeable and experienced they are. What you have to take into account is that there are not always 'rights' and 'wrongs' in this issue.

What works for one person with one particular type of horse might not work for another because there are so many variables to take into account: the job the horse is asked to do and the way he is asked to do it, the rider's abilities and limitations, the horse's conformation and so on. For instance, while we all aim to get our horses working from behind into the hand, some riders like to have a definite contact but others prefer a lighter feel. Horses, too, have their likes and dislikes – never forget that you can read this book and decide that Dobbin should go best in a loose ring, French link snaffle, but Dobbin might not like the weight of this mouthpiece and would prefer a hollow mouth snaffle.

Whether you are a happy hacker, a polo player or a showjumping star, there are some ground rules. First, whatever bit you use, it must be the right size and shape for the horse's mouth and be adjusted correctly. Secondly, it must be one that both you and your horse are happy with: in other words, he must be relaxed and as free from resistance as possible and you must be in control.

Thirdly, there is no such thing as a bit that acts like a magic wand. An old saying states that there is a key to every horse's mouth; there will indeed be a combination of mouthpiece and cheekpieces which will enable you to get better results, but these results can only be achieved when the right rider is in the saddle and the right hands are on the reins. You often hear statements such as 'a thick mouthpiece is milder than a thin one' as if this is a fact written in stone, but the truth is that any bit is only as mild as the hands on the reins. And if the horse is uncomfortable with, for instance, a thick snaffle because the shape of his mouth does not allow enough room for it, it will be a potentially more severe bit than one with a thin mouthpiece.

What you use goes hand in hand with the way you use it. Changing your horse's bit and/or noseband can bring about definite results, but the reins must still be in competent hands. You must also take into account your horse's training (or lack of it!). Do not assume that an older horse is necessarily well educated; a four or five-year-old who has been broken and schooled by a good rider and trainer can be more balanced, responsive and better educated than a ten-year-old who has either never been schooled correctly, or whose schooling has been set back by incorrect riding.

When you want to achieve a certain aim with your horse, or to solve a problem, your choice of bit and tack is an important part of the equation. But it is only part of it: you can use it as an aid to improve the communication system between you, but cannot and should not expect it to work miracles.

Whenever you consider what sort of bit to use, think about your own riding skills and what you are trying to achieve. Always aim to ride from the leg into the hand, thus producing impulsion which the hands contain. If your hands are the dominant factor – if you rely on them to steer, decrease your horse's speed or attempt to get him into an 'outline' – you are, in effect, riding backwards. Forward movement is a vital factor, which is something we all know but often forget. Trying to get a horse on the bit by using your hands to bring in his nose is like trying to drive a car without using the accelerator – neither will work.

Bitting is a subject that provokes a lot of prejudices, which often start out as good intentions. The commonest is that the best bit is always some kind of snaffle – this is

*Some horses may need a change of bit for jumping and working at speed. This onward-bound horse jumps happily in a pelham and stays responsive to his rider, but pulls like a train in any form of snaffle. His saddle is a forward cut general purpose one.*

because we are brainwashed into thinking that snaffles are always mild and therefore always kind to our horses. But there are riders, horses and circumstances that are much better served by using a bit with a curb action, such as a pelham.

It ought to be possible to school just about every horse or pony so that he goes well on the flat, in a confined area, in some sort of snaffle. However, it does not necessarily follow that you can always achieve the same results when riding at speed, jumping or, in some cases, when hacking out. The better a horse's balance and way of going on the flat, the better he will be when jumping, but if enthusiasm or excitement makes him stronger or less inclined to listen to you, you may find that a change of tack is necessary.

Sometimes a different noseband or different type of snaffle does the trick. But if you find that his conformation is better suited to a pelham or kimblewick, why feel guilty? It is far better to use a bit with a degree of curb action gently than to pull at a snaffle. The horse will respect the action of the bit, which when used properly is not at all severe, and you stay relaxed and hopefully ride better because you are not fighting the horse.

Competitors must read the rule books of their particular disciplines to make sure that they do not contravene rules on tack; bits and nosebands are the biggest minefield, particularly in dressage and the dressage phase of horse trials. At Preliminary and Novice level you can use only an approved snaffle – but there are so many on the list that you ought to find something suitable. Showjumping tends to leave tack more to the rider's discretion, though there are still pitfalls for the unwary.

Showing classes also have their own rules, though these tend to be based more on tradition and an accepted idea of what is correct than on hard and fast commandments. Basically, anyone competing in an adult showing class riding anything other than a four-year-old novice should use double reins, which means some kind of double bridle or pelham. Again, there are so many variations on mouthpieces and curb chains that it should be possible to find something to suit every horse.

## Introducing a bit

Many people are nervous about bitting young horses for the first time because they are worried that they might inadvertently damage the horse's mouth. The other headache for many owners who are inexperienced in dealing with young horses is deciding which bit to use. When you pick up a magazine and read that famous dressage rider 'A' likes to use a rubber jointed snaffle because it has a 'softer' mouth than cold metal, but famous dressage rider 'B' hates rubber jointed snaffles because they believe such bits encourage horses to chew the mouthpiece too much, it is hardly surprising that so many people are confused!

While you obviously need to take care that your youngster's early experiences of wearing a bit are as free from trauma as possible, you have to accept that some horses are going to be puzzled or slightly resentful of it at first. After all, you are suddenly asking him to put up with a lump of metal or plastic in his mouth – and his natural reaction is going to be to try and spit it out.

Horses vary in their reactions to different stages of the breaking process. What one finds alarming, another will accept without turning a hair. So while some horses accept the bit as if they have worn one all their lives, other will stay 'mouthy' for quite a while. Understandably, a lot of horses also become mouthy while they are changing their teeth; as a leading horse dentist remarked, life might be a lot easier if we refrained from breaking and riding them until they were five years old and the teething process had finished.

Unfortunately, most of us need to back our horses at three years and expect them to start their ridden work proper at four. It may well be necessary to introduce a bit much earlier than that: if you have a strong two-year-old or even yearling who learns that you have little control over him with a simple headcollar, it is much more sensible to introduce a simple snaffle bit. If you use it with a leading rein and coupling, the horse should not develop a 'one-sided' mouth (as frequently happens when lead reins are fastened in the conventional way and the horse is led more often from one side, usually the nearside, than the other).

Before you introduce a bit, double check that your young horse's mouth and teeth are in a fit state for him to accept it (see Chapter 1). Once you know that he is as

*Some trainers like to use a breaking bit with keys to encourage a dry-mouthed horse to mouth at the bit.*

*This Nathe mullen-mouth snaffle and loose-ring, hollow-mouthed, single-jointed one are both suitable bits for a young horse beginning his education.*

comfortable as possible, introduce it for short periods. Choose some sort of snaffe for simplicity's sake – but the way it fits is more important than its type.

The mouthpiece must be the correct width for the horse and the bit must be adjusted high enough so that he cannot get his tongue over it: once a horse learns this habit, it can be difficult (but not impossible) to cure. Breaking bits were used by most trainers as a matter of course – these have a central link and keys which encourage the horse to play with the mouthpiece and relax his jaw. They went out of fashion in some circles when it was suggested that it was a bad practice to encourage the horse to play with the bit and would make him fussy in the mouth. Such bits are still in favour in many dealing and nagsmen's yards – which, after all, tend to be the sort of places where it is the results that count!

To a certain extent, you have to use your common sense and assess your youngster's reactions. If he is over fussy with a breaking bit, try a half-moon rubber or nylon snaffle or one with a Nathe mouthpiece (a special kind of strong but flexible plastic). Alternatively, a loose-ring, jointed snaffle may give enough play to encourage him to relax his mouth and jaw, but not so much that he is forever fussing with the bit.

Give him time to get used to the idea. Do not put a breaking bit in on Monday, swap it for a loose-ring snaffle on Tuesday and decide to try an eggbutt snaffle on Wednesday. Once you have made your mind up which sort to start with, give the horse three or four days to get accustomed to the idea. If he is not starting to settle, get advice from someone who is used to dealing with young horses on what to try next.

The main things to remember are to be calm, patient and positive and to think ahead – do everything you can to avoid giving the horse an unpleasant experience at this early stage. Remember that he has to get used to the feel of a bit in his mouth. He also has to learn that it is part of a combination of signals that you want him to respond to. When you educate a horse you teach him a new language; put yourself in his place and remember what it was like when you first started learning French at school. The teacher did not expect you to hold conversations right from the start: you learned the basics and built on them.

The same applies here. Your horse has to learn to accept a bit and to respond to it as part of a new language: first he learned to walk on and halt from your voice, now he learns to do it from a combination of voice, legs, bodyweight and rein aids. The more practise you have in using a language, the more proficient you become: at first you have to think about every word, but gradually you become more fluent and your responses become instinctive.

Horses, like people, learn by experimenting. Many 'nagsmen' – people who break and school horses for a living – like to stand young horses in fairly loose side reins for a few minutes before they are ridden; a Schoolmasta (see Chapter 11) could be even better. Correctly adjusted, these will both work on the principle of reward: the horse may put pressure on his mouth, or even catch himself in the mouth by jerking against them, but the important thing is that he is the cause, not the rider. Horses quickly learn that if they do A, the result is B; it does not take long for them to learn that if they accept the bit and relax their jaw, they are more comfortable.

If you have only ridden experienced horses, it can be quite a shock to realise that a young horse's mouth is not naturally responsive to your signals. It will be sensitive in that he will react to discomfort, but you have to 'make his mouth'. Again, this is something that so many nagsmen are good at, and there is no reason why a competent rider and handler cannot achieve similar results.

It is a gradual process that can be arrived at from several directions, including riding, long reining, lungeing, using side reins and work on the ground. You may start by using a combination of all or many of these techniques; the riding will become the most important as the horse's education progresses, but there may still be times when lungeing or long reining can be used to help you work through a problem. (For more advice on introducing your horses to tack, lungeing and long reining, see *Breaking and Schooling* by Carolyn Henderson and Lynn Russell, published by Swan Hill Press.)

## Fitting a bit

It is vital that whatever bit you choose is the right size for the horse and is adjusted to the correct height in the horse's mouth. Many people use bits that are too wide, and often compound the error by adjusting them too low in the horse's mouth.

If the bit hangs too low in the mouth, the horse will often try and put his tongue over it. Some try and do this anyway, for a variety of reasons, but the last thing you want is to encourage the habit or give them an excuse to try. A bit that is too small will pinch the sides of the horse's mouth, causing discomfort – and not surprisingly, the horse is likely to resist the rider's hands.

To measure a bit, lay it on a flat surface. If it has a jointed mouthpiece, pull the cheekpieces out on either side so the mouthpiece is straight. The actual measurement is taken from the points shown in the diagrams.

How to measure a bit

Extend bit to full width before measurement

Bits used to be measured in inches and half inches and could also be ordered in quarter-inch increments to give an exact fit for the horse who did not have a 'stock size' mouth. Nowadays they are often sold in metric sizes – though some saddlers who maintain that these new-fangled measurements will never catch on stick to the Imperial kind! Always take a tape measure with you when buying a new bit, because they do vary slightly, and it is annoying to get your five and a half inch bit home only to discover that it actually has a five and a quarter inch mouthpiece. If you cannot get a metric sized bit to fit, try and get hold of an old Imperial sized one, and vice versa. Just a slight difference in measurement can make a big difference to the fit.

To judge whether a bit is the correct size for a horse, first make sure that the bridle cheekpieces are adjusted so it is correctly placed in his mouth. A jointed bit should wrinkle the corners – though not exaggeratedly so – and a mullen-mouthed bit, such as a pelham, should fit snugly into the corners. Hook your thumbs through the cheekpieces and gently put pressure on each side so the mouthpiece is straight in the horse's mouth. If it is the correct size, there should be about a centimetre's gap between the cheekpiece and the side of his mouth on each side. A rough guide is that you should be able to fit your little finger between the cheekpiece and the horse's mouth on each side – unless you have very large hands!

If you need to measure a horse's mouth, use a piece of dowelling with two martingale stops on it. Place the dowelling gently in the horse's mouth and slide the martingale stops in until they touch the sides of the mouth. Measure between the stops and add half an inch/two centimetres to get a good idea of what size bit you need. If your horse is in between sizes, you will either need to have one specially made or use the nearest size, as long as the discrepancy is miniscule. A bit that is slightly too large and fitted a hole higher, or one that is slightly too small and fitted a hole lower, may work well; avoid pinching his mouth at all costs.

These are the 'textbook guidelines' for measuring and fitting a bit. Horses being horses, you may find the occasional one who does not like things being done by the book! Some horses prefer the mouthpiece to be slightly lower or slightly higher in their mouths; even altering the cheekpiece one hole on one side (and gently evening up the position of the bit) can make a difference to their way of going. Horses who try to lean on the bit sometimes go better if the bit is adjusted a hole higher than normal.

Before using any bit, even a new one, check its condition. It is not unknown for a poor finish or badly made joints to result in tiny sharp edges, which can soon cause discomfort. Check the alignment of cheekpieces with the mouthpiece, too. If a joint is tighter on one side than the other, you could find that the bit is locking or sticking on one side.

## The bit 'families'

Look in any saddler's shop and you will see a bewildering variety of bits. Yet they can all be divided into four basic families: snaffles – with gag snaffles as a farther offshoot; double bridles; pelhams; and bitless bridles. Including bitless bridles might seem like a contradiction in terms, but they are an important part of the 'bit and bridle' picture.

Once you start sub-dividing these families, you run into telephone numbers. For instance, out of interest I started counting different varieties of snaffle – I stopped at 76 and there were still more to include in the list. A well-known loriner (manufacturer of bits and metal fittings) once said, 'Of every twenty bits I make, nineteen are for man's heads and not more than one really for the horse's head.' Perhaps we should all bear that in mind when deciding what to put in our horses' mouths!

Snaffles are in many ways the simplest form of bit because they are usually used with a single rein. Gag snaffles, which should always be used with two reins, are not included in that generalisation.

The double bridle has two bits, one on a separate headpiece called a sliphead. It comprises what used to be called a bradoon (which in modern parlance has become a bridoon, though you will find that purists prefer to stick to the original name) and a curb bit. The two together are often referred to as a Weymouth set, though a Weymouth was originally a particular type of curb.

The pelham attempts to combine the action of both bits in one mouthpiece – and while it may not work in exactly that way, you often find that some horses go very well in such a bit. There are several reasons that may contribute to this; for instance, most pelhams have unjointed mouthpieces and many horses like these. They also learn to back off the curb action slightly, which means that they begin to carry themselves instead of relying on the rider's hands – provided, of course, that the rider remembers to use his or her legs and (you have guessed it) ride from the leg into the hand.

When the horse starts to carry himself, everything begins to feel much lighter and better balanced. The rider then often loses unwanted tension in his or her body, arms and hands. The next step is that the horse says 'Thank heavens you've stopped pulling/ hanging on to my mouth/wiggling on the bit to try and get my head in' and the overall picture becomes much more harmonious. Finally, riders may be much more respectful of what they regard as a stronger and more powerful bit, so they use it with more care.

Bitless bridles can play a useful role, though their use is limited in some forms of competition. Such horses who have bit-related problems can have their confidence restored by these; some can then be re-educated to a bit, while others are always happier in a bitless bridle. Inevitably, bitting problems are caused by people: perhaps physical discomfort or even pain linked to wolf teeth or mouth ulcers has gone unnoticed by an unobservant owner, or a young horse changing its teeth has been labelled as 'stroppy' and been ridden too aggressively.

If a horse is resistant, it shows in his mouth even if the cause of the problem does not rest there. A horse with pain in his back or hock will often be stiff and 'gobby' and will be reluctant to relax his jaw. Unfortunately, riders do not always recognise this and often switch to a potentially stronger bit and/or noseband in an attempt to improve the horse's way of going. Needless to say, the attempt is often a failure.

Horses have good memories. If a horse associates being ridden in a bit with discomfort, he will often carry on associating the two even when the source has been removed. In these circumstances, a bitless bridle can be used either permanently, or until he regains confidence in his rider.

# Chapter 6
## Snaffles

This chapter and the next one look at different types of bits within the main families. Of all the groups, the snaffle family offers more choice – and therefore more room for confusion! However, it is a good place to start.

Bits and bridles act on different 'control points' on the horse's mouth and head: the bars and corners of the mouth, the tongue and, in some cases, the poll and the curb groove. A snaffle is said to act on the corners and bars of the mouth and the tongue, but the actual mechanics vary according to the type of snaffle used and the position of the horse's head. Often it is also said that a snaffle has a raising action while a curb has a lowering effect – but this may be a rather simplistic set of definitions.

A young or unschooled horse will work with a lower head carriage and his nose in front of the vertical. In this situation, a snaffle tends to act in an upwards direction with pressure more on the corners of the mouth than the bars. A well-educated horse or pony who works in a more advanced outline will have a higher head carriage (though the poll should always be the highest point) and his head will be on the vertical. In his case, the bit will act predominantly on the bars of the mouth.

All this, of course, presupposes that the rider is balanced, aware and sympathetic. A snaffle will not act in an upwards direction if the rider's hands are fixed at the withers and 'locking' the mouthpiece. All that is likely to happen then is the horse's head will go up, he will set his jaw against the rider's blocking hands and will either refuse to go forward against them or will pull because of the discomfort.

Nosebands, martingales and training aids or gadgets also have an effect on a bit's action – this is especially true of snaffles. As this book progresses, you will hopefully see that choosing tack is like putting a jigsaw puzzle together: if all the pieces fit, you get the desired overall picture, but if one is missing you end up with a problem.

Two farther considerations affect a bit's action: the mouthpiece and the cheekpieces. The four common types of snaffle mouthpiece are the straight bar, the mullen (or half-moon), the single-jointed and the French link. There are also variations such as mouthpieces with rollers set in or around them and double-joined mouthpieces with half-moon centre links.

The straight-bar mouthpiece is often used as an in-hand bit, but rarely for riding. It acts predominantly on the horse's tongue, but does not put as much pressure on the bars. For this reason, a lot of handlers like it for stallions and youngstock.

Mullen mouthpieces are slightly arched to allow room for the tongue. They have a more definite action on the bars and some horses find them very comfortable. There is said to be a disadvantage in that they do not allow independent rein action – tension on the left rein, for instance, produces pressure which is also felt on the right side of the mouthpiece. But as we are often told that our hands must act to complement each other, so that we have an inside rein and an outside rein acting in partnership, maybe this is really a question of semantics.

Single-jointed snaffles are the commonest kind, but not always the best. They allow a more independent rein feel, and have a squeezing or nutcracker action. The straighter the arms of the mouthpiece, the more definite the nutcracker action.

Some horses dislike single-joined bits and may prefer a double-jointed snaffle such as a French link – this has a kidney-shaped central joint which takes pressure off the tongue. Bits with a half-moon central joint and the Dick Christian snaffle, which has a central ring, also eliminate the nutcracker action.

Do not confuse the above bits with the Dr Bristol, which has a flat-sided central joint designed to put pressure on the tongue. The latter is sometimes useful with horses who become strong in some situations; as long as it is used sympathetically, it can persuade them to listen to their riders a little more closely!

The material from which the mouthpiece is made also needs to be considered. This can range from stainless steel to rubber to plastic, with copper adding another ingredient.

One of the commonest forms of mullen mouthpiece is made from vulcanised (hardened) rubber. This is found in snaffles, pelhams and kimblewicks. It is a thick, heavy mouthpiece – particularly in the snaffle, which is not supported in the mouth in the same way as the other two – so horses tend to either love it or hate it.

Flexible rubber mouthpieces or those made from special types of plastic reduce weight, but are not as resistant to teeth. Rubber snaffles must have a chain-link core so that if the horse does chew through the mouthpiece, you are not suddenly left without any control. These bits wrap round the horse's jaw and can be useful with animals who are frightened of any contact on the reins – but because they have a 'dead' feel, the horse usually soon learns to lean on them.

Nathe snaffles, which are made from a flexible but tough sort of plastic, are a favourite with many leading riders for young or sensitive horses. They seem to encourage the horse to mouth the bit and many that 'back off' from metal snaffles will go up to a contact much more happily with one of these. Other forms of plastic mouthpiece have their devotees, including those marketed as having the taste and/or smell of apples!

Stainless steel is a common material for bits because it is strong and easy to keep clean. Nickel, which was used to make bits and stirrup irons before stainless steel was invented, can bend or break so is not a safe choice.

The one advantage of nickel was that some horses seemed to like the taste – which is why a lot of dealers and 'nagsmen' keep them in their tackrooms. A modern and safer alternative is offered by 'German silver' bits with a high copper content. Copper encourages horses to mouth and salivate, which to a certain extent is necessary if they are to stay relaxed and comfortable. A dry mouth is an insensitive and often uncomfortable one because there is nothing to lubricate the movement of the bit in the mouth and you have metal dragging on flesh.

You can now add to your list of options by deciding what sort of cheekpiece would be appropriate. The four basic types for snaffles are loose ring, eggbutt, full cheek and D-ring. A loose-ring gives more to play on the mouthpiece, as the latter makes constant, albeit small movements in the horse's mouth whereas the others are more fixed and the mouthpiece therefore stays more still.

How do you choose which sort to use? Basically, it depends on the way your horse goes (or does not go!) and the effect and feel you want to achieve. No bit can enable you to counter every one of your horse's evasions, but schooling problems (or challenges, if you prefer to look at them that way) fall into general categories. Initially, work out what you would like to improve, then see which type of snaffle might help you achieve that.

Sometimes the answer might be a combination of tack, so you will also need to consider nosebands, martingales and perhaps training aids.

## Common types of snaffle

The *loose-ring, jointed* snaffle is one with which many horses and riders feel comfortable. There are two types of rings: wire rings, which are mostly common found nowadays, and flat rings. Wire rings are thin and rounded and move a little more freely than flat rings; the latter are often found on older bits rather than modern ones.

The size of the rings varies according to the type of bit. Bradoons have small rings, moving up the scale you have the medium-sized rings of 'ordinary' snaffles, and finally extra large ones on racing snaffles. The idea of the large rings is that they help to keep the horse straight by applying pressure on the side of the face.

Mouthpieces vary from the thin one of the bradoon to fat ones used in hollow-mouth German snaffles. Hollow-mouth snaffles are lightweight and some horses prefer them for this reason.

Many riders like to use rubber bitguards with this and other loose-ring snaffles. These help to keep the mouthpiece central and prevent the rings pulling through the mouth (which in an ideal world would never happen, but in the real one, could). They also remove the risk of the horse's lips being pinched between the rings and the holes through which they pass.

This bit can be a good choice for the horse who is confident to take a contact and benefits from its slight movement. It can help dissuade the horse who likes to lean on

*The eggbutt hollow-mouth and D-ring snaffle both stay relatively still in the horse's mouth, whilst the loose-ring bradoon allows more movement.*

the bit and prefers his rider to hold his head up rather than do it himself, and is also useful for the horse who tries to set himself above the bit. With a fixed bit, such as an eggbutt snaffle, he would find this relatively easy – but because the loose ring snaffle is never static, it makes it harder for him.

Using the same logic, it is often not successful on the horse who is particularly fussy in his mouth, or who repeatedly tries to come behind the bit.

The *loose-ring, mullen-mouth* snaffles are in some ways a contradiction in terms, because the loose-ring is designed to give movement and the mullen mouthpiece is designed to stay still. In practice, you get a combination that some horses respond to very well – a bit that allows just enough movement to avoid a 'dead' feel.

The *eggbutt* jointed snaffle is perhaps the commonest of all, and is often used in riding schools. In this context, it is a very good bit, because it minimises the damage that can be done to a horse's mouth by novice riders. The eggbutt sides mean there is no risk of pinching and if the bit is the correct size, it stays central in the mouth.

Because it stays still (unless the rider has very mobile hands and arms) it is often a useful bit for fussy horses or those who are reluctant to take a contact and go behind the bit. Again, it comes in various sizes and types of ring and mouthpiece, from the eggbutt bradoon to the German hollow-mouth eggbutt.

Some eggbutt cheeks have wire rings, while others have flat ones. In theory the wire rings allow a little more play, but in practice the difference is so slight as to be barely noticeable. Occasionally you see flat-ring eggbutt snaffles with slots in the top of the rings to take the cheekpieces; they seem to be popular in America and would probably find the same acceptance here, if only because we always love to find a 'new' type of bit!

The design of the slot-cheek eggbutt has a lot to recommend it. The mouthpiece is held slightly suspended in the horse's mouth, which many find more comfortable than one which rests on the tongue, and the cheekpiece slots means that rein pressure also applies a little pressure on the poll, thus helping to persuade the horse to lower his head. The hanging cheek snaffle (see later in this section) follows a similar principle.

The eggbutt mullen-mouth snaffle stays so still in the mouth that it suits very few horses – but for those few, it can be a problem solver. This or the loose-ring mullen-mouth snaffle can also be a way to keep inside the dressage rule book for horses who go beautifully in pelhams but hate any form of jointed snaffle. Do as much work as possible in a pelham and switch to your mullen-mouth snaffle for your competing; some horses accept the switch, even if only for a short time.

If you try this, remember that you cannot use a prohibited bit to warm up in and switch to a 'legal' one for your test. Current rules stipulate that only permitted tack can by used anywhere on the competition ground, including the warm-up area.

## Full-cheek snaffles

Full-cheek snaffles are often useful bits for young, green horses – or older, ignorant ones! They can give the rider extra steering power and help to keep the horse straight – as we are all aiming to ride our horses forwards, straight and in balance, that can be very useful. The downside of this logic is that if a horse is teething, the pressure from the cheekpieces can sometimes add to his discomfort. In this case, you will need to use another bit (or a bitless bridle, depending on the severity of the problem) until his teeth have come through and his mouth has settled down.

There are several variations on the full-cheek snaffle, but whichever one you choose, there is a common denominator that is often overlooked. The shape of the cheekpieces must accommodate the shape of the horse's head if he is to be comfortable with this bit; this means that the top 'arm' of the cheekpiece should be angled slightly away from his face.

Unfortunately, some manufacturers do not take this into account, and the result is a cheekpiece continually pressing into the horse's face. This can obviously make him uncomfortable and lead to resistances. Horses with fine, tapering faces and muzzles may not be affected, but those with larger heads – such as cobs and hunters – often are.

Strictly speaking, full-cheek snaffles should be used with leather keepers on the top arms to keep the bit in the correct position in the mouth. However, some riders like to use them without because they feel it allows for more movement. The inherent risk in this is that if the horse learns to grab the bottom arm in his mouth, it could get hooked on his teeth, with disastrous consequences. I know of a case where this happened; the horse reared in pain and fright, went over backwards and landed on top of his rider. If these snaffles are used without keepers, you lose some of the guiding effect of the full cheeks.

When used with keepers, full-cheek snaffles stay still in the horse's mouth. This makes them useful for fussy animals, but non-starters for those who tend to lean on the bit. They are also useful for horses who try to put their tongues over the bit, as the keepers help to keep the mouthpiece high enough.

The classic cheek snaffle is the loose-ring Fulmer, also known as an Australian loose-ring snaffle. This is used in the Spanish Riding School of Vienna, the Mecca of classical horsemanship – which perhaps says it all! As the name suggests, small loose rings are set outside the full cheeks to take the bridle cheekpiece and reins.

This allows a little more play than a fixed cheek, and in some cases makes the difference between a responsive and a 'dead' mouth. It is said that when this bit is used with a drop noseband, a good rider can achieve the same flexion in a well-schooled horse as if they were using a double bridle. The reason is that the keepers give very slight poll pressure and the drop noseband acts in the curb groove.

Full-cheek snaffles with fixed rings sometimes have eggbutt sides, which can lead to the arms being longer. This in itself might not be a problem, but it can become one if the dimensions of the horse's head mean that the cheeks become trapped under a cavesson noseband or the top part of a Flash.

The Fulmer loose-ring snaffle has a single-jointed mouthpiece. Full-cheek snaffles with fixed rings offer a wide choice, including rubber, Vulcanite, nylon or plastic straight or mullen mouthpieces, French links and jointed snaffles with alternate copper and silver rollers set into them (see next section).

There are also half-cheek – sometimes called half-spoon – snaffles available. These have a lower arm only, the bottom part of which is usually flattened into a spoon shape. The idea behind them is the same as the ordinary full-cheek snaffles, to keep the horse straight. They are designed primarily for trotting horses (driving) but are sometimes seen on riding horses.

## D-ring snaffles

D-ring snaffles are also designed to help keep a horse straight, though their action is less positive than that of a full-cheek bit. They can have a slight lifting action, and although logic says that a horse which leans on the bit should not go well in one that stays still in the mouth, this one seems to work very well in some cases.

They are available in several versions, including a single-jointed stainless steel mouthpiece, a single-jointed rubber covered one and a version which incorporates alternate copper and steel rollers. The thinner metal mouthpieces make for a potentially stronger bit, which a lot of horses respect and go well in when used correctly.

The rubber covered version seems to be a 'love it or loathe it' bit – horses that are reluctant to take a contact sometimes gain confidence from it, but a lot of horses give an unresponsive feel. Some horses, particularly young ones, also seem to persist in trying to get their tongue over it even when it is adjusted slightly higher than normal.

Many horses go well in D-cheek snaffles with alternate copper and silver rollers, which encourage them to mouth the bit and relax their lower jaw. It is important to check how this bit wears, because copper is much softer than steel and you can end up with sharp edges.

## Hanging-cheek snaffles

Despite their ominous sounding name, these bits are now permitted in dressage tests. For a long time they were only allowed when used in a bradoon version as part of a double bridle, thinking which had no logic behind it.

At least one manufacturer calls this bit a Filet Baucher. Quite where the 'Filet' comes from nobody seems to know, but Francois Baucher was a French horseman who many experts consider to be one of the fathers of equitation. Referring to them as hanging-cheek snaffles at least removes the risk of butchering the French language!

These bits look like the top half of a jointed pelham, without a curb chain. The bridle cheekpiece fastens to the small top rings and the reins to the larger ones below it; this means that the bit is suspended in the horse's mouth rather than resting in it. Horses who dislike weight or tongue pressure will often take kindly to these bits, which can be found with single-jointed or French link mouthpieces.

The hanging cheeks means that rein pressure also applies poll pressure, thus giving an extra means of persuading the horse to lower his head. As always, it is vital that the rider understands the importance of riding from the leg, into the hand – and understands the difference between a horse being on the bit and merely tucking his nose in.

## The Fillis snaffle

The Fillis snaffle is now rarely seen, but at least one British lorinery company includes it in their catalogue. It was developed by James Fillis, a nineteenth-century horseman whose work *Breaking and Riding* is one of the equestrian classics. In many ways this bit looks very like the hanging-cheek snaffle (hence its position in this section) but there are major differences.

For instance, its use is not permitted in dressage tests – which is another reason why authorities who decide the rules of the sport should perhaps take a long, hard look at its

*The Fillis snaffle (top) and the hanging-cheek snaffle are both suspended in the horse's mouth and minimise tongue pressure. This is particularly true of the Fillis snaffle, which unfortunately is not permitted in dressage tests – though the hanging-cheek snaffle is.*

saddlery regulations. The reason for its exclusion may be that it has a central arch, or port, and is therefore assumed to be potentially severe.

There seems to be a common belief that port mouthpieces are designed to put pressure on the roof of the horse's mouth, which would be barbaric. In fact, they are designed to make a bit kinder and more 'user friendly' by allowing room for the tongue. An exaggeratedly high port probably would cause discomfort or pain, but the one incorporated in the classic Fillis snaffle does not.

The mouthpiece is jointed on either side of the port, so – as with the French link mouthpiece – there is no nutcracker action. A lot of people may not like it, but a lot of horses certainly do.

## The gag and other 'strong' snaffles

If you are looking for the real controversy in bitting, this is probably it. There are many so-called 'strong' snaffles, but the fact remains that in the right hands, used in the right way, they can make for a happy horse and rider – in that order.

All bits have the potential to damage a horse's mouth and should be treated with caution. Those that are capable of exacting greater leverage than 'ordinary' bits deserve even greater respect.

However, there are some bits that are perhaps not as potentially severe as we may think. Some of the roller snaffles are a case in point; so too is the Dr Bristol. If you feel that one of the bits in this section could improve communication between you and your horse, use it under the guidance of a good rider and instructor to start with.

This does not necessarily mean someone with a string of qualifications after their name (with apologies to all the good riders and teachers who are impressively qualified). It may be a showjumper, event rider or whatever who is successful in the sphere you want to succeed in. More often than not, they will also be someone who breaks, schools and often sells horses as part of earning a living.

If you want to use one of these bits, the chances are it is because your horse is too onward bound. At the risk of repetition – and with no apologies for it – remember that your tack is only part of the picture. You must also look at the way you keep and ride your horse.

Is he getting too much high-energy food and not enough work and/or turnout? Is he too big for you? Are you simply not on the same wavelength? A gutsy horse needs a gutsy rider if both are to be happy!

Are you established enough in your riding to be able to get the best out of a forward going horse? Realising that you have to use your legs on a horse who always seems to want to go faster than you do is one of the hardest lessons to learn, but once you have appreciated it you will never forget it.

Is he strong, or is he on his forehand – or is the problem perhaps a combination of both? Changing bits and/or nosebands will not help if you do not know the value of half halts, transitions and other exercises to establish his balance and keep him interested in his work. (*Breaking and Schooling* by Carolyn Henderson and Lynn Russell, published by Swan Hill Press, will give you further ideas.)

## The gag snaffle

The classic gag snaffle, which belongs in a bitting family of its own, requires a bridle with special sliding cheekpieces that run through slots in the top and bottom of the bit rings and attach to the reins. The idea is that pressure on the gag rein lifts the bit in the horse's mouth, thus raising its head. In this way, it gives the rider more control over the horse who has found one of the most difficult of all evasions to overcome – bringing his nose in to his chest and pulling like a train.

There are three essentials to remember when using a gag bit. The first is that you should always use a second pair of reins attached to the bit rings as normal, with the two reins being held like those of a double bridle. A lot of riders are reluctant to do this and ride solely on a gag rein, but this is neither safe nor subtle.

If one of the sliding cheekpieces breaks – and there have been plenty of instances of this happening – you are left with no control on one side. Imagine the consequences if this happened when you were galloping or jumping a big fence.

The second essential is that the cheekpiece should run smoothly up and down the bit rings so there is no danger of the bit locking in position. Some riders believe that rolled leather cheekpieces are best in this respect while others prefer cheekpieces made from cord.

Thirdly, look to your own riding technique. One of the fundamental principles of riding is that as soon as a horse obeys whatever you have asked him to do, you reward him by ceasing to give the command. This means that if you put pressure on the reins and the horse gives to you, you must immediately relax the pressure by the appropriate degree. 'Giving' to the horse does not mean throwing the reins at him!

The riders who use gag snaffles most effectively and whose horses are happy in them are those with balanced seats. This is inevitably accompanied by a stable lower leg position at speed and over fences – look at photographs of top event riders for examples.

If you set your hands against a horse wearing a gag snaffle (or any other bit) you will deaden his responses to its action. This is where riding with two reins on a gag has an added advantage; you can ride as if on an ordinary snaffle and keep the gag rein as the back-up it is intended to be.

Gag snaffles usually have eggbutt or loose rings. Some experts in their use believe that the sliding cheeks run more freely through an eggbutt cheek because there is more stability.

It is possible to use a gag with small rings as the bradoon element in a double bridle – possible, but not recommended. If the rider is this desperate, they are probably beyond help and the horse needs completely re-schooling.

However, occasionally you see this arrangement on polo ponies, usually coupled with a standing martingale. As a gag snaffle has a raising action and a standing martingale is used to prevent the horse putting its head too high, there can be no logic to that at all. Polo is a law unto itself; top players explain that they deliberately over-bit their ponies so that they are always slightly behind the bit and waiting for the command to turn, accelerate or decelerate. Unfortunately, not all players have the skill of the top riders.

Mouthpieces are usually single-jointed, either stainless steel or rubber-covered. You also find them with rollers set round the mouthpiece.

## Roller snaffles

Snaffles with rollers set round or in the mouthpiece are traditionally described as 'strong' bits, though there is no real reason why they should be any stronger than ordinary mouthpieces. They are often more effective, but this is simply because the horse plays with the rollers and relaxes his jaw instead of setting it against the rider's hand, or cannot lean and set himself against a continually moving mouthpiece.

The three common types of roller snaffle are the Cherry roller, the copper roller and the Magenis. The Cherry roller has loose rings, which add to the bit's ability to move, and round rollers, or cherries, set round the mouthpiece. It is fairly fat and heavy, which makes it a good choice only for a horse who is happy with a bulky mouthpiece.

Those who go better with a thinner one often prefer a mouthpiece with alternate copper and metal cylindrical rollers. Copper is supposed to make a horse salivate; this, coupled with the mobility of the rollers, makes it difficult for the horse to lean on it.

Bits with this sort of mouthpiece inevitably have either full or D-cheeks; occasionally you see a Fulmer loose-ring snaffle with a copper roller mouthpiece. In the case of the first two, it

*Roller snaffles are sometimes useful for horses who need to be encouraged to mouth the bit – or discouraged from trying to lean on it. The D-ring snaffle with alternate copper and steel rollers and the Cherry roller both have rollers set round the mouthpiece, while the Magenis snaffle has rollers within it.*

might seem illogical to have a mouthpiece that encourages mobility coupled with cheeks designed to promote stability, but the fact remains that some horses go well in these bits. The slight lifting action of the D-cheeks may help to discourage the horse from leaning.

The Magenis snaffle has rollers set inside the mouthpiece rather than round it. The arms of the mouthpiece are often squared off rather than rounded, which gives more positive pressure and increases the bit's potential strength. Again, a lot of horses like it – or at least, respect it and go happily in it.

The one thing that does make these bits potentially stronger than 'ordinary' snaffles is that the mouthpiece arms are straight, not slightly curved to allow for the shape of the jaw. The nutcracker action is therefore a positive one.

## The Dr Bristol

The Dr Bristol is often confused with the French link snaffle, as both have a central link. But whilst the French link's central plate is kidney-shaped, to take pressure off the tongue, the Dr Bristol has a flat plate to put pressure on it.

Sometimes a strong horse will back off and listen to his rider when a bit feels different. This is often where the Dr Bristol scores, and a lot of experienced riders like to have it in reserve for jumping or hunting. Keeping a horse thinking is part of the battle – and if changing between two or three bits helps, why not?

Some people maintain that this bit has no right or wrong way up, but it is better to be safe. Hold the bit in front of you as if it were in position in the horse's mouth: if the top of the plate is angled towards you, it is the right way up, but if the top of the plate slants away from you, it is upside down.

The Dr Bristol mouthpiece can be incorporated with eggbutt or D-cheeks. The latter may be slightly more positive, because of their lifting action.

## The three-ring snaffle

This bit is known by lots of names, including the Dutch gag, the Belgian gag, the Continental snaffle – even the fat lady bit! It first became popular a few years ago on the showjumping circuit and was dismissed by many people as 'just another showjumpers' gimmick'. However, its use became more widespread and a greater number of riders started to appreciate its versatility.

The bridle cheekpieces fasten to the top ring, thus giving poll pressure in the same way as a hanging snaffle or a pelham. You have the choice of three rings on which to fasten the reins; the lower the ring, the greater the leverage it is possible to obtain. If you use the bottom ring, be aware that the leverage is potentially very powerful.

As long as the horse is ridden correctly, this bit can help show him how to work in a round outline, with his hind quarters underneath him. If he is ridden incorrectly, in

*Some horses prefer a double-jointed mouthpiece to a single-jointed one. The Dr Bristol (top) gives tongue pressure and is thought of as a 'strong' snaffle, while the French link has a kidney-shaped central plate which minimises tongue pressure. The French link is a permitted bit for dressage, but the Dr Bristol is not.*

other words with too much hand and not enough leg to create impulsion coupled with half halts, etc, he will simply learn to bring his head in and his nose down and will bumble along on his forehand – thus creating even more problems.

Some of our top showjumpers are still the real experts at using this bit. In some yards, it has replaced draw reins (another controversy, another story and another chapter). They start off by working a horse with the reins on the second or lowest rings; when they have established the shape and way of going they want, the reins are moved to the top ring to reward the horse and check that he is in self carriage.

Before condemning this, remember that expert showjumpers are not looking for the same things as expert dressage riders. The latter wants to satisfy a judge with a classical way of going; the former wants an athletic horse who can turn against the clock and still leave the poles up.

*The three-ring snaffle gives varying degrees of poll pressure, depending on which rings the reins are attached to. If they are used on the bottom rings, there is the potential for a lot of leverage.*

It does not matter if the horse is overbent or behind the bit; our expert showjumper wants his horse to stretch along his topline while he is warming up, put his hind quarters underneath him and be in a physical and mental state to lengthen and shorten his stride, turn, accelerate and decelerate as soon as his rider presses the buttons.

Inevitably, there will be less than expert showjumpers trying to use the same equipment and techniques to get the same effect, but without the same success.

## The American gag

Sometimes called a Tennessee Walking Horse bit, this has a sliding cheek and is potentially more powerful than the three-ring snaffle. It can be used with two reins or with a single rein on the bottom ring.

As with most bits, it has its place in the right hands. In the wrong hands, it can do a lot of damage. I know a leading veterinary centre which received a hard-pulling horse for treatment after a day's hunting. His weighty male owner had put all his strength against that of the horse – and fractured the horse's jaw, which counts as cruelty even if it is accidental.

*The American gag has a similar action to the three-ring snaffle, but has sliding as opposed to fixed cheeks.*

## The Wilson and Scorrier (or Cornish) snaffles

These snaffles are similar in design and action but differ in the nature of their mouthpieces. The Wilson snaffle, designed primarily as a driving bit, was the forerunner. Like the Scorrier, it has two pairs of rings attached to a single mouthpiece; the bridle cheekpieces attach to the inside set and the reins to the outside one.

When pressure is put on the reins, the result is an inwards squeezing action. The Scorrier works in the same way, but usually has wire rings instead of flat ones and often has a mouthpiece that is twisted on one or both sides. One well-known event rider describes the Scorrier as 'the stop anything snaffle' – but unlike most of us, he has the riding ability and the good hands to use it.

## Conclusion

The snaffles covered in this chapter are not the only ones available. There are a few that would better be described and kept as curiosities, such as the chain snaffle – simply a length of chain between two cheekpieces. Contraptions like this are scarce, but the few that remain should be preserved – not because they are useful pieces of equipment, but as a reminder of the inhumanity riders have been known to sink to.

*The Waterford snaffle has a multi-jointed mouthpiece. It is often thought of as a strong bit, but some horses go nicely in it.*

There are also snaffles that may work with some horses and some riders, but are not of wide enough use to count as a mainstream bit. The Waterford snaffle, sometimes referred to as the 'bobble bit,' is an example of this. Snaffles with twisted mouthpieces have been excluded deliberately because their potential for bruising the bars of the mouth is so great.

The Chifney bit must not be ignored – but you could not call it a snaffle, nor is it a curb. In fact, it is a real odd man out in that it is used not for riding but for leading. Sometimes called an anti-rearing bit or colt leading bit, it was originally designed to give handlers of highly strung colts and stallions more control when their charges tried to rear. It looks like a squashed metal ring with a straight bar along the top, two small rings at the side and a third underneath.

It is fitted so that the straight edge acts as the mouthpiece, with the rest of the bit encircling the horse's jaw. The bridle cheekpieces fasten to the side rings and the leading rein to the bottom one. Potentially, it gives a lot of leverage on the horse's bottom jaw and must be used with care. However, horses respect it and it can make the difference between being able to handle a horse and having no control. A lot of professional transporters will use a Chifney on a horse who is difficult to load.

Finally, there are the real 'experts only' jobs such as the Citation. This combination of a special bridle and a bit with two mouthpieces was used with great success by event rider Ian Stark on the equally talented Murphy Himself – one of the most talented and reputedly the strongest horse ever to power round a three-day event.

The trouble with this type of tack is that the likes of you and me see partnerships of the above sort using it and wonder if it will work for us. The brutal but realistic answer is – no, because our ability does not match that of Ian Stark and our horses (unless we are very lucky) do not have the power and courage of Murphy Himself.

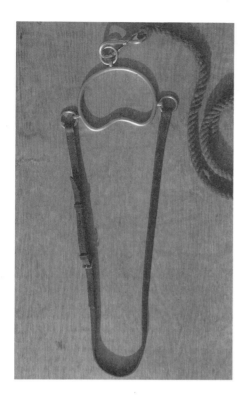

*A Chifney is used for leading rather than riding and is also known as an anti-rearing bit.*

As saddlers know to their cost, riders are quick to emulate the famous. Admittedly that is not necessarily a bad thing, especially if you model your showjumping style on the Whitakers or your cross-country technique on that of Mark Todd or Lucinda Green.

But do not assume that a piece of tack will work for you because it works for them. One saddler still shudders every time she hears the name of Eddie Macken – not because she had anything against the talented Irish showjumper, but because of the 'Boomerang craze'. Eddie rode Boomerang in a bitless bridle, which led to a steady stream of children wanting 'a bridle like Eddie Macken's'. She solved the problem and kept her conscience clear by selling them cheap sheepskin sleeves for their ordinary nosebands: the children were happy and the ponies suffered no ill effects!

# Chapter 7
## Doubles, Pelhams and Bitless Bridles

In the right hands, the double bridle allows a rider the ultimate opportunity to communicate with their horse. In the wrong hands, it causes even more problems than those which its user presumably hoped it would correct.

The double bridle should not be used to force a young or uneducated horse to work in an 'outline'. Sadly, many people use it with this in mind, particularly in the show ring. The same applies to the double as to the pelham – it can be used as a quick method of getting the horse to tuck his nose in, which to an uneducated eye may look as if he is on the bit. But as a horse is truly on the bit only when he is working from behind into the rider's hand, pulling in the front end and expecting the rest to follow does not work.

Nor should it be used to give extra brakes, in the sense of the rider who believes that if they pull hard enough on the curb reins, the horse will stop. Often the reverse will happen: horses do not back off from pain, they run away from it, so a horse that pulls will often pull harder in an incorrectly used double bridle.

However, if it is used correctly on a horse whose education means he understands and is capable of responding to the rider's aids, the double bridle gives extra control in the best sense of those words. The horse will have the confidence to relax his jaw and carry himself, with his hocks and quarters propelling him forwards and the energy contained lightly by the rider's hands. An experienced and competent rider may use it to re-school a difficult horse, but only if or when that horse understands what is being asked of him.

It is very easy and convenient to say that a double bridle works on the principle that a snaffle (in this case the bradoon, or bridoon) raises the horse's head and the curb lowers it. But as the late Anthony Crossley, one of the most influential authorities on British dressage, maintained with such logic – that argument is too simplistic to hold water.

A snaffle can be used to ask the horse to lower his head just as effectively as it can to ask him to raise it. Mr Crossley told us to think of the snaffle in terms of restraining and steering. He believed that if the horse's systematic training meant that he carried his head more or less on the vertical, the snaffle would rest in the correct place on the bars of the mouth and the horse would work comfortably. The horse's head would naturally be carried according to its state of balance: raising or lowering actions would not really be part of the equation.

How does the curb bit work in the context of the double bridle? Mr Crossley believed that the purpose of the curb was to encourage the horse to relax his jaw, which would

*A well-fitting double bridle. Compare the bridle on this show hack, with its padded noseband and coloured browband, with the plain bridle on page 92. The hack bridle would look out of place on a cob or hunter.*

set off a series of responses. The culmination of this would be a balanced horse ready to respond to the rider's aids.

A curb may sometimes have a 'lowering' effect on the horse's head carriage to the extent that rein pressure also gives pressure on the poll. However, with some horses it may simply encourage them to tuck their noses into their chests, keeping their heads as high as before. When this happens, it is often due to the rider using too much hand and not enough leg. There is also the occasional horse who dislikes poll pressure and fights it no matter how effective and sympathetic the rider.

If you want to see a curb used kindly and to full effect, watch leading exponents of the art of Western riding. Their horses are as light and balanced as most Grand Prix dressage horses – and perhaps better than some!

These riders rely on a combination of bodyweight, leg aids and neck reining – bringing the rein to the neck to indicate bend and direction – to achieve the skilled manoeuvres necessary for cutting cattle, etc. A good Western partnership can turn on the proverbial sixpence, move sideways at an equally impressive rate and perform a sliding stop with ease.

The horses are often ridden on no more than the weight of the rein. They respect the curb, but have complete confidence in it. It is a pity that Western riding is sneered at as 'cowboy tricks' by some people – yet often those who dismiss it are struggling to achieve any degree of lightness in their horses using a snaffle.

## Fitting a double bridle

It is obvious – but unfortunately often overlooked – that a horse can only be expected to be comfortable in a double bridle if his mouth has enough room to accommodate two bits. This has nothing to do with the size of the horse; a 14.2hh show pony may be quite happy in a double, whilst a 16.2hh heavier type may find it literally too much of a mouthful. Generally, horses with a higher percentage of Thoroughbred blood are less likely to have problems than those of predominantly cold blood.

This is one reason why show hacks, which are predominantly Thoroughbred or Anglo-Arab, often go happily in double bridles, while show cobs – whose lineage, if known, is very different – usually go much better when ridden in pelhams. However, some cobs and many hunters can accommodate a double bridle if enough care is given to the choice of bits and curb chain.

A double bridle should be fitted so that the bradoon is as high in the mouth as is comfortable for the horse. Loose ring bradoons are used most frequently, though the horse who prefers a bit to stay still in his mouth may go better with an eggbutt. Hanging cheek bradoons are also available.

The curb should fit neatly into the corners of the mouth and the curb chain should rest in the curb groove, in front of the bradoon. Start by adjusting the bradoon, then adjust the curb so that it sits immediately below it. As a rough guide, you should just be able to fit two fingers between the front of the bradoon and the back of the curb, at the side of the mouth. Always take great care in fitting and adjusting a curb chain. If it is twisted, or adjusted too tight or too loose, the horse will be uncomfortable and may show this in no uncertain terms.

Start by attaching one of the end links to the offside curb hooks. Then standing on the horse's nearside, twist the chains to the right (clockwise) until it is flat and the fly link – the centre link through which a lipstrap is passed – hangs down. Hold the chain in your right hand with your fingers between it and the horse's jaw and your thumb on the outside of the last link. Slip the last link onto the nearside curb hook, keeping your thumbnail up and the link turned in a clockwise direction. If the chain is too loose, select the correct link to give you the right amount of adjustment and slide that onto the nearside hook – but this time, keep your thumbnail down and turn the link anti-clockwise. This will keep the links flat.

The curb chain should come into contact with the horse's jaw when the curb cheeks are drawn back to an angle of 45 degrees. If it is too loose, the bit cheeks will come too far back and interfere with the action of the bradoon; if it is too tight, it will come into play too soon. Riders who are nervous about using a double bridle for the first time often adjust the curb chain too loose in the mistaken belief that they are being kind to their horses. A curb chain that is so tight that it presses continually on the horse's jaw will obviously cause him discomfort and in bad cases will lead to rubbing and soreness.

Strictly speaking, a lipstrap should always be used when a bit employs a curb chain, though some people do not bother. It does help to keep the chain lying flat – and if you are carrying a bridle with the curb chain unhooked, fastening the lipstrap means you are less likely to lose it. Curb chains have a habit of falling off, usually into long grass on a showground. The lipstrap should be loose enough not to put pressure on the curb groove, but not so loose that it flaps about.

## Double decisions

When deciding which type of bradoon and curb to use, one of the most important factors is the dimensions of the curb bit. As it works on a lever principle, it follows that the longer the curb cheeks, the greater the leverage available. In the days when each horse had his bits made especially for him, much greater choice was available; these days, there are usually just two options.

The standard length of curb cheeks, from top to bottom, is usually the same as the width of the mouthpiece. In other words, a five and a half inch mouthpiece will have five and a half inch cheeks. This seems to work well in most cases. Horses who are particularly sensitive and 'back off' a standard curb bit too much may be more relaxed with a Tom Thumb curb. This has shorter cheeks and often does the trick, especially if used with an elastic or leather curb 'chain'.

The length of the cheek above the mouthpiece is usually half that of the cheek below it. Again, this equation seems effective and comfortable for most horses. If the upper cheek is proportionally longer, the poll pressure will be greatly increased and a lot of horses will resent it.

Curb cheeks can be either fixed or sliding. The latter allows a little more movement of the bit in the horse's mouth, but also more leverage. Therefore, it is potentially a little more severe, but some horses seem to relax their jaws more with a sliding cheek curb. It is very much a case of trial and error: as always, start with a short-cheeked curb that is potentially the mildest and try others if this does not seem to have the desired effect.

The shape of the mouthpiece must also be taken into account. Most curbs have a port, a slight arch in the centre designed to make room for the tongue. This is not, as many riders imagine, a severe piece of design – unless it is exaggeratedly high and coupled with long cheeks. In this case, it would be possible for the top of the port to come into contact with the roof of the horse's mouth, which would be unforgivable.

Curb mouthpieces can be fat or thin. The general rule applies that the fatter the mouthpiece, the greater its bearing surface – but as with snaffles, there are some horses who do not like bulk in their mouths. When you are asking a horse to cope with two mouthpieces, that rule applies even more strictly.

Most curbs are variations on a standard design. The Banbury curb, though, is something of a loner, and in skilled hands can suit horses that dislike 'ordinary' curbs. It has a round mouthpiece, usually tapered in the centre to give room for the tongue, and is designed so that the mouthpiece can revolve as well as slide up and down. This means that it is continually moving in the horse's mouth, which some prefer.

## Curb chains

The permutations which can be obtained through different types of curb are increased when you take the curb chain into account. Curb chains in the pure sense are made from stainless steel links and can be either single or double; the double link is more flexible and therefore potentially more comfortable for the horse. Some horses respect and are comfortable with the definite but not rough action of broad, flat-linked curb chains; these are an old design and may be difficult to find these days.

Rubber curb chain guards are designed to soften the action of the chain still further, but are unattractive. When used in situations when appearance is important, such as in a show class, the effect is similar to a woman in a beautiful dress and wellington boots. If you want a very mild curb action, choose a leather or elastic version – many light-mouthed horses go just as well in these as with the conventional chains.

A special bonus should be on offer for the modern bit manufacturer who comes up with a better design of curb chain hook than the standard one. No matter how careful you are, it is sometimes difficult to keep them laying flat to the horse's face – and their bearing surface is so small that they have the potential to rub. A curb hook with a small flat backing plate would be much more comfortable for the horse.

## Holding and using double reins

Many riders shy away from the idea of using two reins because they feel they will not be able to manage them. In fact, it is similar to riding a bicycle – once you are

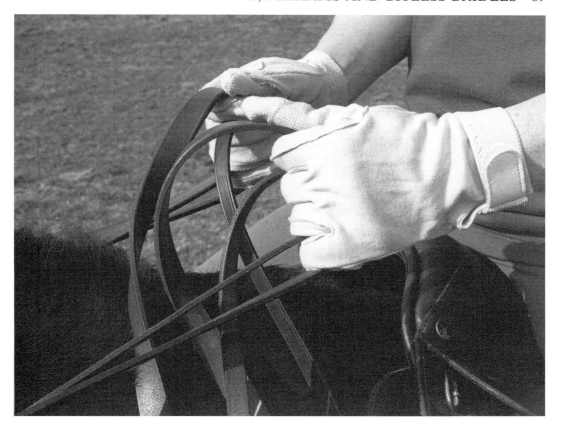

*The most usual way of holding double reins.*

confident and have the knack, you wonder how it could ever have seemed complicated.

First of all, decide which rein is required to have the dominant action, because that will be held on the outside. Most often, and certainly if you are just starting to use double reins, the top (bradoon) rein should be the outside one. There are several ways of holding double reins, but the most usual way is to hold the top and bottom ones on each side in separate hands.

The bradoon rein passes beneath the little fingers and the curb reins go between the third and fourth fingers. Both pairs then pass through the hand and come out on top of the first finger, with the thumbs on top. However, if you separate them so that the bradoon rein is on top of the first finger and the curb rein goes between the first and second finger, again with the thumb on top, you will have a much greater sensitivity. Once you have tried the second method, you will find that the first one feels like playing the piano with gloves on!

Riders at the Spanish Riding school often use another method of holding double reins. Although it again requires separate hands, it means that the bradoon rein is even more dominant and the curb acts on little more than the weight of the rein. For this technique, hold both curb reins and one bradoon rein in one hand and only the bradoon rein in the other.

Finally, if you have a very powerful horse who likes to bore down on the rein, you can hold the bradoon rein between the first finger and thumb with the curb rein under the little finger. This method actually has much to recommend it: holding the bradoon rein between first finger and thumb often gives a more sensitive feel and can be used just as well with a simple snaffle rein. The reason must be that we use our thumbs and first fingers more than our fourth finger – perhaps we would all be better riders if we either improved the dexterity of our fourth fingers or held the reins as just suggested. One well-known showjumping trainer used to make riders on his clinics do just that if he thought they were too ham-fisted.

## Pelhams

Pelhams are much maligned bits that deserve wider appreciation. Purists dislike them because their logic is faulty, but in practical terms they have a lot to offer. Trying to combine the action of a separate bradoon and curb in one mouthpiece means you inevitably end up with imprecision, but these 'blurred edges' can be an advantage in some cases.

When a pelham is used with two reins, the theory is that the top rein has a snaffle action and the bottom one, that of a curb. In practice, you get either a very small amount of leverage, poll pressure and curb action from the top rein or markedly more from the bottom one. Because both are attached to the same mouthpiece, the pelham can never have the independent actions of the double bridle.

Riders who feel that two reins are too much of a handful, especially for jumping, often opt for leather couplings called pelham roundings. These link the top and bottom bit rings and mean that only one pair of reins is needed. This gives an action somewhere between the two, but you lose the flexibility which double reins offer.

Some horses who lack confidence in other bits – which may be due to the bit, the rider or both – respond well to a pelham. Once you have made the initial breakthrough with a pelham, you can often change to some form of snaffle with success if you need to. A few years ago a dealer friend had an Irish horse in her yard who had a reputation of being 'a strong ride' – often an Irish euphemism for a puller – even in an enclosed area. The horse had great potential as an eventer, but did not co-operate when asked to do his flatwork and dressage tests in a snaffle.

He was ridden for six weeks in a vulcanite pelham with metal curb chain and became a much lighter, more responsive ride. When a vulcanite loose-ring snaffle was substituted for the pelham at his dressage tests, he still went beautifully. The snaffle was kept purely for dressage tests; at home and in showjumping and cross-country competitions he continued to work in his pelham. This combination of lateral thinking and gamesmanship saw the horse progress to intermediate level before he was sold abroad to continue his eventing career.

Many people believe that a pelham, especially one with a broad, mullen mouthpiece like the vulcanite pelham, will encourage a horse to lean on the bit. In fact, the reverse is often true. It may be that he learns to respect the different pressure points or that his rider uses the bit more sympathetically. Possibly he was leaning to avoid discomfort – a horse will not back off from discomfort or pain in his mouth, he will pull or lean harder to get away from it and deaden the sensation.

The design of the mouthpiece and cheekpieces, plus the choice of curb chain, affect the way a pelham can act. As with a curb, you usually find that the length of the cheeks equals the size of the mouthpiece, so a five and a half inch bit will have cheeks which also measure five and a half inches. This usually works well enough, but if your horse needs a six inch bit and you do not want that amount of potential leverage, your supplier may have to make a bit specially for you. This will not be a problem for a good lorinery company, who can combine existing cheeks and mouthpieces, but it will be more expensive than an 'off the shelf' bit.

When deciding which sort of pelham to try, take your horse's conformation into account. If he has a thick tongue and/or a short mouth, a very thick mouthpiece may be uncomfortable for him. Although some people will tell you that it is more severe (which is debatable) a mouthpiece with a small port may suit him better. This small arch in the centre of the mouthpiece allows room for the tongue.

Horses with long mouths and tapering muzzles, such as many Thoroughbreds, may not be as suited to pelhams as they are to double bridles. This is because a single mouthpiece means that the reins can never be truly independent, and the curb chain tends to slide out of the curb groove on this sort of horse and act on the jaw – which is uncomfortable for the horse.

There are many varieties of pelham, some better known than others. The commonest is the vulcanite pelham – or to be more exact, the mullen-mouthed pelham with vulcanised rubber mouth, which is the modern equivalent. If you find an old fashioned vulcanite pelham, perhaps at a sale, buy it even if you do not need it at the time: vulcanite is also a form of hardened rubber, but some horses prefer it to the modern versions. A mullen mouthpiece is usually better than a straight bar one, as it has a gentle arch which allows room for the tongue to fit underneath.

Horses who dislike the bulk of a vulcanite snaffle may prefer a stainless steel mullen mouthpiece. Next step on is the Cambridge mouth pelham, which has a ported mouthpiece. Horses which dislike pressure on their tongues often go well in this version.

*A hunterweight double bridle with various types of pelham. Clockwise, from the top, are a Hanoverian pelham with Rugby cheeks; a Rugby mullen-mouth pelham; a Hanoverian pelham; a Vulcanite mullen-mouth pelham and a jointed pelham.*

The above three pelhams are the ones in commonest use. However, there are many others that have a useful role and are often found in specialist showing yards – though if more riders were aware of them, they might be more widely used. For showing, it is usually correct for the horse to be ridden in double reins, but not all horses (or riders!) are happy with a double bridle.

When this happens, some form of pelham provides a good alternative. The Rugby pelham, which has separate 'bradoon rings', allows a little more play on the mouthpiece and also gives more distinction between the bradoon and curb actions than the fixed-ring pelhams. If a separate bridle sliphead is used on the bradoon ring, as with a double bridle, it gives a more finished appearance to the horse's head which is appreciated by many showing exhibitors. The Rugby pelham usually has a ported mouthpiece, though it is possible to find mullen-mouth versions.

Occasionally, a horse with fleshy lips may suffer rubs from an ordinary mullen-mouth pelham. If this happens, try a Scamperdale: the mouthpiece bends back at each end, which means that the cheekpieces are kept away from the mouth.

The Hanoverian pelham has a ported mouth with rollers round it. The idea is that these encourage the horse to mouth and relax his jaw, and in the right hands it can have a good effect. However, it should only be used by a rider with an independent seat and good hands, as most versions have longer than normal cheekpieces which are capable of exerting a fair amount of leverage.

The SM pelham – named after Sam Marsh, a horseman who used it to great effect – is another pelham in the specialist category. It has a broad, flat mouthpiece with a port which allows room for the tongue, but its real effectiveness stems from the hinged sides. These give independent rein action and mean that the bit stays in the correct place in the horse's mouth however he carries his head. Again, it is a pelham for experienced and sympathetic hands.

The jointed pelham rarely seems to give satisfactory results, mainly because the curb chain does not act as well as it does with an unbroken mouthpiece. However, if you remove the curb chain and curb hooks altogether you have a snaffle with a similar action to a three-ring or Continental one.

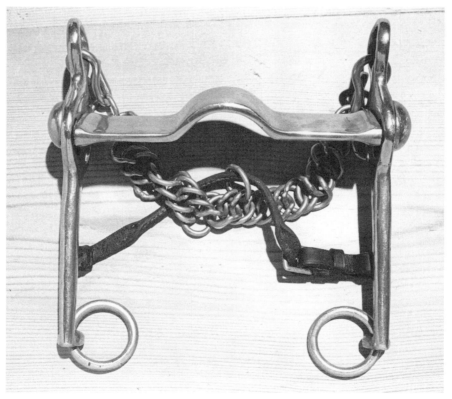

*The SM pelham, named after the man who popularised its use, Sam Marsh. It has hinged sides, which give an independent rein action, and a mouthpiece which gives room for the tongue and stays at the correct angle however the horse holds his head. This pelham is fitted with a lipstrap.*

## The kimblewick

The kimblewick is related to the pelham but is only used with one rein. In theory, it acts like a snaffle if the rider's hands are held relatively high whilst a curb action comes into play if the hands are lowered. The exception is the kimblewick with flat, slotted cheeks: if the reins are fastened to the top slots you get a theoretical snaffle action and if they go to the lower ones, a curb action supposedly predominates.

In practice, the cheeks of a kimblewick are capable of so little leverage that it is like riding on the top rein of a pelham. The position of the hands does affect the action of the bit, but this also applies to a snaffle. As with the pelham, there is poll pressure because the cheekpieces fasten on to rings at the top of the bit. This is made more definite if they are squared off; these days, most are rounded.

Like pelhams, kimblewicks are available with a variety of mouthpieces. Most have a small port – though mullen-mouth versions are available – and there is also a jointed

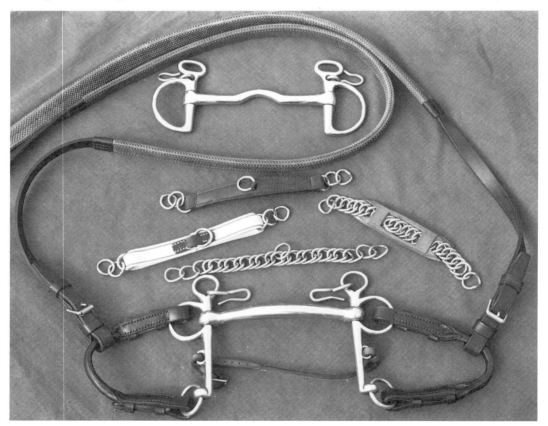

*A kimblewick (top) and a mullen-mouth stainless steel pelham fitted with pelham roundings and a single rein. These reins have buckle fastenings, which are safer than billet fastenings and thus preferred for jumping and racing – billet fastening are more usual in the show ring. The different curb chains are leather, elastic, metal and metal with a rubber guard.*

kimblewick. The curb action of the latter is so limited as to be not worth bothering with, but if you remove the curb hooks you have a hanging snaffle.

All horses and riders are individuals, and it is dangerous to make sweeping generalisations about a subject as controversial as bitting. However, I have never known a horse that did not go better in a pelham with two reins than a kimblewick.

## Bitless bridles

Bitless bridles are colloquially called hackamores, which drives purists to distraction – a hackamore is actually a particular type of Western bridle. However, it is a term that has passed into common equestrian usage and is likely to stay.

A hackamore should be in every tack room because if you do not have one, the chances are that a situation will arise when it could make life much easier. Most of us use bits without thinking of alternatives unless we have to, and worry that any system that operates without something in the horse's mouth must mean the rider has less control.

This is not true – especially if you are having problems because your horse resents or is uncomfortable with his bit. A horse who has been educated to accept a hackamore will go as obediently and comfortably as one who has been trained with a conventional bit; problems arise only if riders expect to put on a hackamore and be able to ride straight out of the yard and round a showjumping course.

You have to accept that if you change to a hackamore, you are using a different control point – the nose. Admittedly this will be one that the horse will, to some extent, be used to – having been led from a headcollar and probably lunged from a headcollar or lungeing cavesson – but you still have to practise to make sure you and your horse are talking the same language.

Riding with a bitless bridle is very good for most of us and can be something of a salutary experience. You may *think* that you use your legs and bodyweight more than or as much as your hands, but the reality is often different. A hackamore teaches you how to place less reliance on your hands, and the beneficial effects can last when you put the horse back in a conventional bridle.

Start by finding somewhere safe to practise, preferably a fenced-in schooling area and definitely not on the roads. Unless the horse is schooled Western style and goes on the weight of the rein, you will hold the reins as you would with a snaffle bridle and have a light contact with the horse's nose.

Begin in walk and find out how to turn by looking in the direction you want to go (which will shift your bodyweight without deliberate action). Discover how to halt by sitting slightly more upright and not following the horse's movement any more. If you do this when you ride with a bit, all well and good: unfortunately a lot of us forget the basics as we become supposedly more 'advanced'.

*A German pattern bitless bridle. This event horse performs his dressage test in a snaffle and showjumps in this bridle. For the cross-country phase, when his owner says he likes to 'grab the bit and go' he wears a roller mouth snaffle with a gag action.*

Gradually move forward to trot and practise upwards and downwards transitions and half halts. As you and the horse become more confident in each other, try the same in canter. You may well find that he starts to come 'on the bit' – or at least, he would if he was wearing one!

It just goes to show that being on the bit is perhaps an unfortunate phrase that concentrates our attention on our hands. What we should really be thinking of is riding the horse in balance, so that he steps through from behind, his back stays soft and supple and he flexes at the poll.

Riding dressage figures, or even a pretend dressage test, in a hackamore can be great fun. It can also be a great leveller when you realise that perhaps you have been wiggling your hands to try and get your horse on the bit, or turning from the reins. Try it and see: it can do your riding a lot of good.

There are times, of course, when using a bit makes a horse uncomfortable. If he is teething, or has an injured mouth, a hackamore can enable you to carry on riding him without making the problems worse. It can also help in re-schooling a horse who has been abused; a lot of so-called pullers have been made that way by riders who hang on to their mouths or even yank at the reins.

To re-school a horse, start off with a bitless bridle as above. When he has relaxed and is going well, fit a simple snaffle such as one with a Nathe mouthpiece and continue to ride on the hackamore, so that the bit is completely passive.

The next step is to ride with a second pair of reins to the bit. Hold the two pairs as if they were on a double bridle or pelham, with the hackamore rein as your dominant rein. Think of the bit rein as one to the curb, and keep a very light, 'barely there' contact: all your signals should still be made from the hackamore.

As the horse's confidence increases, you should gradually start using the bit rein, very tactfully. If the horse becomes tense or resists, use the hackamore rein instead. It can be a slow process, but in most cases it works.

If the horse settles in a hackamore but just will not accept a bit, you will have to stay with the former. Unfortunately, it is not acceptable for showing or dressage, though you can use it for showjumping and even cross-country if you have the confidence. Should your sights be set on a discipline where a bit is mandatory, your only options are to persevere, with expert help – or to sell the horse to someone who is happy to ride in a hackamore.

## Types of bitless bridle

The simplest form of bitless bridle is easily put together at home. Fit a snaffle bridle with drop noseband, minus a bit, and fasten a narrow pair of reins to the rings of the noseband. This is not recommended as a permanent set-up, but can be useful if you want an idea of how your horse would go in a hackamore (or are brave enough to put your riding to the test and find out how much you rely on those reins).

The commonest types of 'proper' hackamore are often known as the English and German hackamores. They are two versions of a type of bridle called the Blair's pattern, and have a noseband attached to cheekpieces of varying length. These operate on a leverage system and are complemented by a strap or chain which rests in the curb groove.

The 'English hackamore' has shorter cheekpieces than the 'German hackamore'. Both, but in particular the German version, are potentially powerful pieces of equipment and should be respected as such. The nosebands, and sometimes the curb straps, are often padded with sheepskin to minimise the risk of rubbing or pressure sores.

If you have not used a hackamore of this type before, get expert help in fitting it. The noseband should be fairly snug, as should the curb strap or chain, and it is usually fitted at about the same height or slightly lower than a cavesson noseband. It is a good idea to alter the height slightly every now and again – a single hole is enough – so that you vary the pressure points.

The Scawbrig is the ideal bitless bridle for re-educating a horse with mouth problems. It comprises a standard headpiece, browband, cheekpieces and throatlatch with a padded noseband which has a ring at each end. A piece of padded leather with tapering ends fits in the curb groove; the ends either continue to become reins, so that the curb groove strap and reins form a continuous piece of leather, or fasten to a conventional pair of reins.

The noseband is fitted as the front of a drop noseband should be, so that it cannot interfere with the horse's breathing, and the bridle works via pressure on the nose and curb groove. To use a bit at the same time, simply fit an extra sliphead.

Finally, there is the Distas pelham (sometimes called the WS bitless pelham, which is even more of a contradiction in terms). This has a padded noseband, metal cheekpieces and curb chain or strap; its strong point is that it is used with two pairs of reins, the bottom one giving more leverage.

# 8
# Bridles, Nosebands and Martingales

Ready-made bridles are usually sold in either pony, cob or full sizes. If your horse has average proportions, you may find that one of these is perfectly adequate; unfortunately horses, like people, do not always measure up to average standards. Too many people use bridles that do not fit properly, which can lead to discomfort and resistance.

There are two ways around the problem of the horse who does not have an 'off the peg' head. One is to have a bridle made especially for him and the other is to mix and match parts to suit his conformation. A bridle comprises five parts: headpiece, browband, a pair of cheekpieces, noseband and reins. You may find, for instance, that by combining a full-size headpiece and browband with cob-size cheekpieces and noseband you are able to get the right fit for a horse with a broad forehead and relatively narrow nose and muzzle.

A made-to-measure bridle is not always as expensive as you might think. If the bridle maker comes out to you, takes all the necessary measurements and makes you a hand-stitched bridle from best quality leather, you will have to be prepared to pay two or three times the price of a machine stitched, mass produced one.

However, a good retailer should be able to help by ordering you a bridle made to your measurements from one of the big manufacturers. You can also ask reputable mail order companies to quote you a price: a certain well-known one charges only 10 per cent more for made-to-measure bridles than standard ones.

A well-fitting bridle is one that is comfortable for the horse. Starting at the top, this means that the headpiece and browband do not pinch the base of his ears; the part of the headpiece which goes over the poll must be long enough before it splits into cheekpieces and throatlatch and the browband must be wide enough to avoid pressure but not so wide that it flops up and down. Pinching browbands are often an unrecognised cause of head tossing.

When the throatlatch (which for some reason is pronounced throatlash – one of those eccentricities of which the horse world is so fond) is adjusted correctly you should be able to fit the width of your hand between it and the horse's face. If it is too tight, it will interfere with his flexion and if it is too loose, it will flap about.

The cheekpieces should allow you to adjust the bit to the correct height in the horse's mouth. To be aesthetically perfect – and this is usually only possible with a made-to-measure bridle – the buckles of the cheekpieces and that which adjusts the height of the noseband should be level with each other and with the horse's eyes.

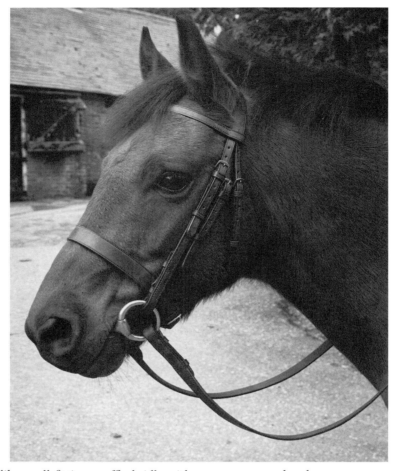

*A workmanlike, well-fitting snaffle bridle with a cavesson noseband.*

Most people prefer to use a noseband, though racehorses are often ridden without. The fit depends on the type and its action, though it should never rub the horse's cheekbones or interfere with his breathing.

You have to decide which weight of leather would suit your horse and your purpose best, as well as what size he needs. Do not fall into the trap of thinking that a lightweight bridle will refine a heavy head: the result will be like an elephant in a tutu. A plain, no nonsense bridle with a flat noseband and browband will make the horse look much smarter.

All bridles should be workmanlike, even the finer sorts worn by show hacks and Arabs. Some of the rolled leather bridles made for Arabs are so fine and must have such a low breaking strain that you have to wonder if they are really safe.

The weight of a bridle is determined by the width of the cheekpieces, with other parts in proportion. Hunters, cobs and half-bred-type horses look best with three-quarter inch cheekpieces – most saddlers still work in Imperial measures for leatherwork even though loriners often follow metric measurements. Those with more Thoroughbred blood look nice with half-inch cheekpieces.

Whether you follow the traditional showing guidelines or add fancy touches is down to personal choice. Tradition dictates that brass clincher browbands belong only on driving horses and that velvet coloured browbands, bound in two or three colours of ribbon to complement the horse's coat, are the province of hacks and perhaps riding horses.

Padded nosebands and browbands, with or without fancy stitching, are not acceptable for hunters and cobs but may be chosen for Thoroughbreds and Arabs with finely chiselled heads. Some dressage riders follow the Continental enthusiasm for black bridles with white piping along the edges of the browband and noseband, and often carry the theme through with white tape on the horse's plaits and white numnahs or saddle cloths.

Years ago, cheekpieces and reins were always stitched to bits. Nowadays stitched fastenings are rarely seen, though you may find them occasionally in the show ring. Modern fastenings can be either hook stud or buckle; the former are neater but arguably not as safe, particularly on reins.

## Synthetic bridles

Synthetic bridles have not won such wide acceptance as synthetic saddles, mainly because mass-produced leather bridles are within most budgets. The world of endurance riding proves the exception to this rule; they have taken to synthetics in a big way, and some of the best types have been designed by leading endurance riders.

The best synthetic bridles are made from hard wearing materials that do not rub the horse – which could be the difference between winning and losing on a top ride – and are easy to keep clean, usually needing only a wipe with a damp cloth. They often come in bright colours, which traditionalists dislike, but somehow fits the cheerful, friendly image of endurance riding. Bright colours must also be safer for riding on the roads: be seen, be safe is a good motto.

Synthetic bridles usually have buckle fastenings and the best convert to a headcollar. This enables the rider to slip the bit out of the horse's mouth to encourage him to drink, then put it back in with the minimum of fuss to continue the ride.

## Nosebands

Most nosebands are designed to help overcome problems, such as horses who open their mouths to evade the action of the bit, those which cross their jaw with the same aim and others which pull or become too strong for the rider to remain easily in control.

Used and adjusted correctly, they can be very useful – but they can also cause more problems than they solve.

We should not assume that a horse must keep his mouth shut all the time. We want him to have a relaxed jaw and to accept the bit, which means that he has to flex his jaw and mouth the bit gently. If his jaws are locked shut by straps of leather, how can we expect him to do either?

Obviously there is a big difference between the horse who mouths the bit and the one who opens it wide and sets himself against the bit. But again, it is important to find out *why* he is evading so strongly. Check for obvious reasons, such as sharp teeth and mouth injuries – and if he is teething, accept that he is bound to go through a difficult stage because he is uncomfortable. If necessary, switch to a bitless bridle for a while.

You also have to take into account that mouth evasions are not always caused by mouth problems. A horse whose back hurts, or who has a hock problem, or whose rider takes a contact which is too strong, will find it uncomfortable to go forwards – and one of the ways he is likely to show this is by raising or tossing his head, leaning on the bit or refusing to take a contact, opening his mouth and generally being 'gobby'.

However, there are lots of horses who discover that if they open their mouths, they can avoid doing what they have been asked to. In this case, once physical problems have been ruled out and you are sure that it is not your riding which is at fault, a change of noseband may help.

The simplest type of noseband is the cavesson, which is often thought to be of mostly cosmetic value – somehow, a horse without a noseband always looks as if he is only partly dressed. Yet there can be more to the simple cavesson than looks.

The textbook fitting for this noseband is that it should be adjusted about an inch below the bottom of the cheekbones and fastened tightly enough to allow two fingers between it and the horse's face. However, if it is adjusted to allow just one finger's width and dropped down a hole or two lower, it can often help discourage a horse from opening his mouth too wide.

In theory, one of the nosebands with a strap below the bit should be more effective in persuading a horse from opening his mouth too much. In practice, the occasional horse hates the feel of even a drop strap that is not too tight, and will simply find another form of resistance. Horses, unfortunately, do not read books like this!

As only a cavesson noseband can be used with a double bridle, adjusting it this way can be a helpful form of persuasion. There is also a variation on the cavesson which doubles back on itself and can be fastened quite tightly without the risk of a buckle digging into the horse's face. This is marketed under various names, mainly the cinch noseband and the doubleback cavesson.

If you want to use a standing martingale, it should only be fastened to either a cavesson noseband or to the top part of a Flash. Never fasten it to any kind of drop strap, which will restrict the horse's breathing – however much of a good idea that might seem in times of duress!

Occasionally you will see horses wearing nosebands with sheepskin sleeves. These have always been common in the racing and trotting worlds, and are supposed to stop horses shying at their shadows. Some people also believe they encourage a horse to lower his head to see over the top of it, hence their popularity in jumping circles.

There are three types of noseband which act both above and below the bit: the drop, the Flash and the Grakle. The drop noseband is the classic design, but went out of fashion for a few years. Fortunately a lot of riders have now recognised its values and it is back in favour. Fashion has a lot to answer for!

The action of a drop noseband is more definite than any other. If the horse opens his mouth too wide, the noseband puts pressure on his nose and on the curb groove; his reaction is usually to lower his head, which means that the bit stays in the correct place and the rider is more likely to stay in control. It is often effective on horses who come above the bit, as long as this evasion is not a reaction to discomfort in, say, the back.

The riders of the Spanish Riding School in Vienna use the combination of a drop noseband and Fulmer snaffle because the extra control points allow them to ask for flexion that is believed to be otherwise possible only with a double bridle. Their ability as riders and trainers may, of course, have rather a lot to do with it!

This noseband should be fitted with great care. It must be high enough above the nostrils not to interfere with the horse's beathing – allow three inches as a guideline. The back strap should rest in the curb groove and be fastened to allow two fingers to be inserted between it and the horse's head, and the straps which go over the horse's head must not rub the cheekbones. If this happens, it is often because the front strap is too short: look for a different fit or ask your saddler to make you a noseband which adjusts on the front as well as at the back.

A drop noseband will only fit correctly if the small rings on the front have spikes which are sewn into the front and head straps. These keep the front strap in the correct position and stop it from dropping down.

The Flash noseband, named after a showjumper, was originally invented so that the rider could use a noseband with some form of drop action and a standing martingale. Standing martingales are not as popular as they used to be, but the Flash noseband is seen more frequently than any other.

Many riders are reluctant to ride a horse in a snaffle bridle and cavesson noseband, which is a pity if the horse goes well in them. They like the extra control of a Flash – or the feeling that they have extra control, because in many cases it is unnecessary and simply acts as a security blanket.

That is not meant to imply criticism of the many riders who use a Flash for definite reasons. There is one school of thought which says that it is useful because it helps keep a snaffle central in the horse's mouth, and another which works on the theory that if it is not needed, the horse will not know it is there.

*This horse wears a Flash noseband and a breastgirth.*

The Flash has a higher control point and a less definite action than the drop, so some horses may accept it more readily. However, it only works if it is made with a substantial cavesson – flimsy ones are dragged down by the bottom strap, which lessens its efficiency and looks awful.

Adjust it so that the cavesson strap is stable, which usually means tight enough to allow one finger between it and the horse's face. The drop strap should allow two fingers. If you really want to, you can also put a sheepskin cover on the cavesson!

The Grakle noseband was originally designed for a hard pulling Grand National winner of the same name. Sometimes called the crossover or figure-of-eight noseband, it has a higher control point than the Flash or the drop and is designed to give more control over the horse who tries to cross his jaws.

*This bridle has a Grakle noseband. Strictly speaking, the browband is too big but this is preferable to one which is too tight and pinches the base of the ears. The horse also wears a running martingale.*

It must be fitted so that the round piece of leather through which the straps cross, which is usually backed with a small piece of sheepskin, is on the centre of the horse's face, halfway between the bottom of the facial bones and the nostrils. It should be snug but not too tight: start by allowing two fingers' width between each strap and the horse's face and tighten it slightly if necessary.

The main area of controversy with Flash and Grakle nosebands is whether they should be used only with snaffles or whether it is legitimate to use them with bits which have a curb action, such as pelhams.

The purist answer is that if you use a curb chain and a drop strap, the latter will interfere with the action of the former – so it should really be a noseband only for snaffles. However, a lot of top event riders and showjumpers find these nosebands suit their purposes when used with pelhams and kimblewicks.

## Less common nosebands

The above three nosebands are the most common in use, but there are others. The Kineton or Puckle noseband and the Australian cheeker are interesting because they do not work on the principle of preventing the horse from opening his mouth too far.

The Kineton consists of a noseband with a metal U-shaped loop at each end. These go around and under the snaffle rings – it should not be used with a pelham or kimblewick, as the bit cheeks and Kineton rings could get caught up, with disastrous results.

When pressure is put on the reins, it is also transmitted to the nose, which in theory encourages the horse to lower his head and 'come back' to his rider. It should be fitted so that it is at the same height as a correctly-fitted drop noseband, and used with caution – in the wrong hands it could easily bruise a horse's nose.

The Australian cheeker, seen most often on the racecourse, is said to have a more psychological effect than a practical one. Made from a single piece of rubber, it comprises bit guards which link to a central strap running down the middle of the horse's face and fastened to the bridle headpiece.

The idea is that the horse can see the central strap and regards it as a 'psychological barrier'. This might sound far fetched, but racehorse trainers are usually pretty down to earth, and enough of them believe in its efficacy. At the very least, it can do no harm – which is more than can be said for other items of tack in the wrong hands. The Australian cheeker can also be used with horses who put their tongues over the bit, as it helps keep the mouthpiece at the correct height.

Finally, if you really want to be obscure, ask your saddler if he stocks nose nets – not to be confused with fine-mesh devices designed to help some head shakers. If you live near Newmarket or other racing-orientated areas, you might actually find them stocked as standard equipment. These wide-mesh net bags go over the horse's nose and fasten to a cavesson noseband; the idea is that the horse backs off from something which makes contact with his nose, thus dissuading him from pulling.

## Reins

There are so many different types of reins designed to give the rider better grip that plain leather ones – which are actually nice to use on a well-schooled horse – are rarely seen on snaffle bridles. They are still most people's choice for double bridles or pelhams used with double reins, especially in the show ring, though some riders prefer a laced or plaited leather bradoon rein; watch a class of big, powerful hunters showing off their gallop and you can understand why!

Whatever sort of reins you choose, make sure they are the right length. Pony reins are shorter, and it is dangerous for children to use longer ones meant for horses. It is too easy for them to put a foot inadvertently through the loop, with disastrous consequences if they fall off.

Another safety move which is often forgotten is to knot your reins at the buckle end if you are riding cross-country and likely to encounter drop fences. This means if for any reason the reins are pulled out of your hands, there is less risk that the horse will put a foot through them and fall.

Reins are still made with a centre buckle, though there is no reason why they should not be a continuous length of leather – in fact it would actually be more sensible in most cases. They were originally made with buckle ends so that the reins of army horses could be linked. It is hard to think of circumstances where today's riders would need to do that, but the tradition lives on even though there is no practical reason for it.

Reins can be stitched to the bit, or have loop, hook stud or buckle fastenings. Stitching is impractical if you want to change bits on a bridle; loop fastenings, where the rein doubles back through a keeper, are uncommon and put a lot of strain on leather and stitching.

Buckles are safest under stress. Hook stud fastenings are fine for most purposes and are preferred by most riders because they look much neater: buckles fasten on the outside whereas hook studs fasten on the inside.

Choosing reins is very much a personal choice. Plain leather looks nice and means there is less bulk in your hands, but can become slippery when wet – either from rain or sweat. Laced and plaited leather gives more grip; plaited leather is difficult to clean thoroughly and can stretch, which makes laced leather the best bet in most circumstances.

Reins with rubber grips give the best security and are universally used in racing. They are also popular for eventing, hunting and showjumping. Their disadvantages for some people are that they are quite bulky, which makes them difficult for children and adults with small hands to use, and are not exactly attractive.

The original rubber covered reins used a reddish rubber which is still common. Brown or black rubber to match the leather looks smarter and you can also buy reins with white rubber grips. These, like white rubber bit guards, look smart to start with but soon become grubby.

Half-grip reins, with rubber along the inside only, offer the best of both worlds in some cases. Originally designed for dressage, they offer the smartness of leather with an improved grip.

If you are buying rubber-grip reins or half-grip reins and know you will need to knot them at the end, check that the buckle ends of the reins before the rubber handgrips start are long enough for you to do so – many are not.

*Plain leather, rubber covered, laced leather and Continental reins.*

Continental web reins are especially popular with showjumpers. These are made from cotton webbing with leather stops sewn along them to prevent them slipping through the rider's hands. Some people like them, but others find that they do not allow a precise enough positioning of the hands. It is also possible to have leather stops sewn along plain leather reins.

Plaited nylon reins in bright colours were bought by the ton when they were first developed in the 1960s, but were so prone to slipping and stretching that they soon went out of favour. Plaited cotton reins are much nicer to use, but are not always easy to find.

## Martingales

Martingales, like Flash nosebands, are used as a matter of course by many riders. This is justified by the argument that if the horse goes well, the martingale has no effect and it only comes into action if the horse tries to evade. This sounds convincing until you take the martingale – whether it be a standing or running type – off a horse who wears one all the time and ride him without.

Often, you will find that rider, horse or both has been using the martingale as an end in itself rather than as a means to an end. Even fitted correctly, it can fix the horse's head carriage rather than him developing true carriage; take it off and you may find that what you thought was a well-schooled horse is rather wobbly and unsteady.

The trouble is that we have come to think of martingales as standard items of tack rather than as gadgets – and a martingale is really just as much a gadget as a pair of draw reins, even if you prefer to call it an 'artificial aid'. Used correctly and in the right circumstances, martingales are extremely useful. Used all the time, they can mean that every time you school your horse, you are conning yourself that he is going well.

It is no coincidence that martingales are not allowed in dressage tests. If you need one for jumping, for hacking out an unpredictable or spooky horse, for schooling a problem horse or for any other reason, then by all means do so. But if you do not know why your horse wears one, take it off and see what happens!

Just because your horse's previous owner rode him in a martingale, there is no reason why you should do so. Similarly, there is no hard and fast rule which states that martingales must be used for jumping. Many of the top American showjumpers ride their horses without martingales, and their free way of going and ability to use themselves with maximum athleticism is very impressive.

Familiarity breeds contempt, and if you use a martingale all the time there is a risk that you and your horse will become dependent on it. Try compromising by taking it off for schooling and see if your horse works as nicely on the flat without it, or if you get problems.

Should problems arise, is it because he does not understand what you are asking him to do, or finds it difficult? You might find that a little expert help can make a lot of difference to his way of going, and that you can save your martingale for the times when you really need it. In some cases, you may discover that once you have sorted out your communication breakdown, these times are few and far between.

The two main types of martingale, standing and running, each have their advantages and disadvantages. When considering whether to use a martingale and deciding which one to choose, it is most important to remember the martingale should be used only to prevent the horse holding his head above the angle of control – not to strap it down. If you try to tie a horse's head down he will only fight even harder.

The standing martingale, which attaches to the girth at one end and a cavesson noseband (or the cavesson part of a Flash) at the other, used to be much more popular than it is now; its advantage in some cases is that it is independent of the reins, so cannot interfere with the horse's mouth. This means that you can use an open rein, which is possible but more limited with a running martingale.

The main disadvantage is that some horses find it easy to set themselves against a standing martingale and use it as something to lean on. If this happens, it is often worth trying a standing martingale with a rubber insert: in Newmarket, at least, these are known as Newmarket martingales because of their popularity in the racing world. The martingale gives an extra degree of control, but the strong rubber has a small amount of give.

Some people dislike the standing martingale because they believe it restricts the horse's head over a jump. But if it is fitted correctly, this should not happen: when a horse is in the air, his head should go forwards and down, not up. If he does throw his head up, the martingale may help to persuade him that this is not a good idea (and also prevent him from banging the rider in the face).

The textbook fitting allows you to push the martingale up into the horse's gullet. You may find it is more effective in some cases if it is adjusted a hole shorter, but it should not need to be any tighter. You should be able to get a hand's width between the neckstrap and the horse's neck.

It is important that a rubber stop is used to prevent the martingale sliding through the neckstrap. If it is allowed to run free, there is a danger that the horse could put a leg through it when jumping or messing about.

The running martingale fastens to the girth at one end and splits into two narrow straps, each with a ring at the end, at the other. The reins pass through the rings, so the martingale obviously has a direct effect on the horse's mouth. This is not always a bad thing: because a running martingale helps to keep the bit in place, it can protect the horse from the effects of unsteady hands.

At one time it was commonly used with two reins, a practice which has a lot to recommend it. If these are held like the reins of a double bridle, with the martingale rein as the bottom rein, it allows you to ride on the free rein and take up the martingale one if needed. You can therefore use an open rein when needed.

It might be worth trying this method if you are nervous about riding without a martingale. It gives you the security of knowing it is there if you need it, plus the chance to find out how your horse goes without it having so much influence.

To fit a running martingale, fasten it to the girth and stretch it out under the horse's neck. When the rings reach the angle of the gullet, where the head meets the neck, you should have a good fit.

This method works better than the classic one of stretching the martingale along the horse's shoulder until the rings reach the withers. All this does is follow the line of the shoulder, when it is the length of the neck that counts.

The running martingale should also be used with a rubber stop at the junction of the neckstrap and martingale body. It is also vital to use stops on the reins, to prevent the rings sliding down and catching on the bit rings. Even worse, there have been cases of horses getting the rings hooked on their teeth, rearing in panic and going over backwards.

Some horses have the habit of grabbing at the martingale straps – a good reason for persuading youngsters that picking up everything from brooms to headcollar ropes in their mouths is not a good idea. Never smack a horse on the head for doing this, or you will make him headshy; say 'No!' in a sharp voice and remove the hopefully undamaged object. If he insists on chewing his headcollar rope when he is tied up, following this with a quick jerk on the rope reinforces the message.

For safety reasons, a lot of experienced trainers like to use a bib martingale rather than an ordinary running one on young horses. Here the straps are joined together by a triangular piece of leather. It should be fitted following the same guidelines as for the running martingale and can, of course, also be useful for older horses who are confirmed strap grabbers.

If you want to use a running martingale with double reins, you must have problems! In all seriousness, a horse that needs a double bridle or a pelham and a running martingale needs some serious schooling by an experienced rider.

In many cases, the martingale is not actually needed but is there as a psychological safety valve for the rider. Be brave: ride without it, in an enclosed area to start with, and you may well find that you do not actually need it.

If you cannot do without it for the time being, many experts believe it should be fitted so that the curb reins go through the rings. This follows the school of thought which says that a snaffle raises the head whilst a curb lowers it – which as has been discussed earlier, is a grey area. If you do this, fit it on the loose side to start with: the last thing you want is for the martingale to lock on to a rein operating a lever effect. If the horse is unhappy and you still cannot bear to ride without it, use it on the top rein instead.

It is possible to buy combination martingales which give the actions of both a running and a standing. These definitely come into the 'over the top' category.

There is another form of martingale which can be more subtle and effective than any of the above – the Market Harborough. As it is actually a combination of a rein and a martingale, you will find it in Chapter 11. In the right hands, it can do a lot of good and does not deserve the reputation for severity that is often put on it.

Last and also least, the Irish martingale has a curiosity value if little practical use for most people; it is rarely seen anywhere outside of racing. It is not really a martingale at all – simply a strip of leather with a ring at each end through which the reins pass. The idea is that if the horse has a fall, it will prevent the reins going over his head.


## Bit accessories

By now it will be obvious that the choice of bit, noseband and – if used – martingale is a recipe which depends for success on the right mix of ingredients. Their effects are inter-related, so it is important to look at the overall picture.

There are also a few small but often useful items to remember. The first are rubber bitguards, sometimes referred to as rubber biscuits: these are large rubber circles with small holes in the centres which fit over the bit rings and act as a cushion between the bit and the horse's face. Their main purpose is to remove any risk of a loose-ring snaffle pinching the sides of the mouth, but they can be used with just about any bit to minimise rubs.

Their second use, which is often not appreciated, is that they help keep a bit central by limiting its sideways movement; this applies particularly to loose-ring snaffles. At the same time, they help to give a more definite steering feel by putting gentle pressure on the side of the face.

Many people struggle unnecessarily to fit them to a bit, especially if it has large rings. There is no need – all you have to do is soak them in hot water for a little while to soften the rubber, then slot two thin straps such as spur straps through the centre hole to give you some leverage. Hold one strap against the bit whilst you pull on the other and the disc will slip over the bit ring quite easily.

Ordinary bitguards are very different from the rather unpleasant devices called brush prickers or cheek prickers. These fit between the bit and the horse's face and have short bristles which press into the sensitive skin; the idea is that if the horse pulls to one side or is difficult to turn one way, fitting a brush pricker will persuade him to change direction. If a horse is that difficult to steer, chances are that he is unbalanced/unschooled/has a physical problem which needs sorting out rather than a set of bristles pushed into his face.

One of the most infuriating problems to overcome is the horse who tries to or succeeds in putting his tongue over the bit. This means that there is no 'cushion' under

*Rubber bitguards mean there is no risk of a loose-ring snaffle pinching the corners of the horse's mouth. This horse – the four-year-old from page 10 – wears synthetic brushing boots with Velcro fastening in front, and leather ones with strap and buckle fastenings behind.*

the bit and although he does not seem to realise it, the horse is actually making himself more uncomfortable.

It is first important to work out why he does it: start by checking for mouth problems such as sharp teeth and ulcers, not forgetting to examine the tongue and inside the cheeks. Some horses start the habit because the bit is adjusted too low, and can be cured simply by fitting it at the correct height or, if necessary, a hole higher. Others do it because they dislike a single-jointed snaffle, and changing to a mullen-mouth or French link one makes a difference.

Alternatively, try using a full-cheek or Fulmer snaffle with keepers on the cheeks. The keepers mean that the joint is kept at an angle higher than normal, which some horses prefer. This may not work if a horse is teething and does not like the pressure of the cheekpieces.

I once had a horse who I bought as a three-year-old, just backed. Unfortunately, his previous owner had used a bit that was too big, and in just a few weeks he had learned to roll back his tongue. He stopped and went quite happily when bitted with a correctly fitted snaffle with alternate copper and silver rollers; he seemed to like the feel of the rollers in his mouth and relaxed. Later, because this is not a permitted bit for dressage tests, he accepted a lightweight, loose-ring bradoon.

Some racehorse trainers use tongue straps, which literally tie the horse's tongue to the bottom jaw. They are only used for a few minutes at a time, but the risks are obvious and they are not recommended.

Rubber tongue ports are a much more humane alternative. This fastens around the centre of the mouthpiece and lies on the tongue, facing back towards the throat. It works very well on some horses, but others manage to manoeuvre it to one side and carry on as before! In this case, a metal tongue grid fastened to a separate sliphead may help.

Every good dealing and training yard has a butterfly or nagsbutt bit, a snaffle which incorporates a metal tongue plate. It is fitted so that the plate lies to the back and will usually prevent the horse getting his tongue over the bit. Some may resent it – and will show their resentment by not going forwards or, even worse, by rearing.

Many people will tell you that the best way to stop a horse getting his tongue over the bit is to keep his mouth shut with a tight drop noseband. A *correctly fitted* drop or Flash may help in some cases, but if a horse manages to get his tongue over the mouthpiece and cannot get it back under, he may react quite violently.

# Chapter 9
# Basic Training Equipment

As soon as you buy a horse, you will start parting with your money to buy tack and equipment. Even if he is an unbroken youngster that you intend to educate, the list will seem endless – headcollars, lungeing and long reining equipment, travelling gear, rugs and so on.

It is always sensible to buy the best quality you can afford. Many people take the attitude that any old thing will do when you are dealing with a growing youngster, because the rug that you buy this year will be too small next season, but this can lead to all sorts of problems.

A rug that 'just about fits' can cause rubs and pressure points. An old bridle with cheekpieces that are wearing through at the holes might seem as if it is worth keeping 'just for lungeing', but if it breaks at a vital moment you could have a panicking horse and a hiccup in your training.

The only safe way, unless money is no object, is to steer a middle course. Forget about the expensive wool travelling rug with your initials in one corner until your horse has stopped growing, but buy or borrow an alternative that does the job and fits well.

Buying second-hand can be a good idea if the equipment is only going to be used for a limited time, or has had limited use, but it must be cleaned, checked over and any repairs made before it is used. If you do not know who they came from – and sometimes even if you do – second-hand rugs and rollers can harbour skin infections, such as ringworm. When in doubt, leave well alone – or at least treat everything with a good anti-fungal product made especially for equestrian use.

If you have the money in the first place, it is often better to buy new and sell later. Equipment that has been well looked after will always find a buyer and you will be able to sell it with a clear conscience.

## Foal slips, headcollars and halters
Most experienced breeders introduce foals to wearing foal slips – lightweight headcollars suitable for their size and weight – within 48 hours of their birth. The reasoning behind this is that the sooner the foal gets the idea of being led beside his mother, the better: they grow in size and confidence amazingly quickly, and the last thing you want is an argument with a bolshy 'baby' who is quite big enough and strong enough to win.

*An adjustable foal slip.*

The foal slip is very basic, and should preferably be made from leather – this will break if it gets caught up, whereas nylon might not. It comprises a headpiece and noseband, both of which should preferably be adjustable and which link to a ring at the back of the jaw. A diagonal strap runs from one to the other, across the foal's face, and keeps the slip stable. Many designs have a strap attached to the back ring which is supposed to be used to lead the foal, but this is not actually a very good idea.

Experienced handlers usually start teaching a foal to lead by holding a tea towel or something similar around its neck – never tied on, in case the foal gets away and the

*A fly fringe fastened to a leather headcollar provides extra protection in summer.*

cloth gets caught up on something. Handlers with a real knack, which comes usually from years of experience, often manage the foal alone by holding the tea towel in one hand and putting the other arm round the quarters. The arm round the quarters is used to gently push and encourage the foal to follow his mother – who is being led by an assistant – while the tea towel helps to steer. If you are not so experienced, it is a good idea to use three people to teach the foal how to lead: one at the front end, one at the back and a third to lead the mare.

Once he gets the idea, you can introduce leading from the foal slip. At first, it is safer to run the leading rope through the back of the foal slip, rather than clip it to the ring; if the foal does get away, there is then no risk of a dangling rope catching round his legs and tripping him up. Once the lesson has been learned, the rope can be clipped in place.

Lead ropes and reins should always be clipped on so that the smooth part faces the back of the horse's jaw and the side which opens is away from it. This means there is no danger of the clip opening and fastening on the horse's face: if this happens, it can cause a nasty injury.

Also for safety reasons, do not use leadrope clips to fasten the door bolts of clever horses who can open them with their lips. If the clip goes into the horse's lip, the resulting injuries can be very unpleasant.

As soon as your youngster is big enough to wear a proper headcollar, invest in one made either from leather or which has fittings designed to break if the webbing straps become caught up on something. The universal nylon headcollar is useful on well-behaved, mature animals under supervision, but should not be worn while they are turned out. Horses have a knack of getting themselves into trouble: I know of a very sad case where a two-year-old caught his nylon headcollar on a gate fastening, perhaps when scratching his face against it, and panicked. The nylon did not break, but his neck did.

In general, it is better not to turn out a horse in a headcollar unless there is a good reason for it – such as him being difficult to catch. Large studs often use headcollars with nameplates on youngstock so they can be identified easily; obviously this only works if you can be sure that the right headcollar goes on the right horse to start with!

Some horses are particularly bothered by flies in late spring and summer. A fly fringe, fixed to a leather headcollar, can afford some relief. A few people save money by making their own: lengths of string attached to an old browband are just as effective as bought fringes.

Fly protectors which cover the ears have become popular over the past few years, particularly amongst showjumpers. However, they are used by some riders not just to keep the flies off but as 'ear defenders' – it is said that horses who object to crowd noises at shows are calmer when wearing fly hoods. Some riders also employ cotton wool ear plugs for horses sensitive to loud noises, but this does not always work: some horses are irritated or even more worried by them.

Turning out is one of the rare occasions when using a headcollar made from cheap leather can be a good idea. It does the job and saves your smart, top quality one getting rained on/rolled on/chewed by other horses in the field!

The best headcollars are adjustable on the nose and at the side of the head and have buckle fastenings. The slip fasteners, which look like buckles without teeth and incorporate a centre bar to lock the strap in place, never seem as satisfactory. If you want to be really smart, you can have a brass nameplate engraved with your horse's name fixed to the headcollar.

A headcollar needs adjusting as carefully as a bridle. The top edge of the noseband should be about two fingers' width below the face bones, so there is no danger of them being rubbed, and if he is being turned out in it you should be able to fit three fingers' width between the noseband and the horse's face. If the noseband is any tighter, he will not be able to eat with it on.

Every well-mannered horse should be obedient to lead in a headcollar – but on the road a bridle is *always* essential – and should allow himself to be caught and tied up. Unfortunately, not all horses are well mannered and you have to be more devious than they are! 'Control' headcollars and accessories, quick-release headcollar ropes and techniques to help you cope with horses who are reluctant to lead, be caught or tied up can be useful in some circumstances. Most control headcollars work by tightening on the poll and/or nose when the horse resists, then slackening again when he submits to the handler. They should only be used for leading, never for tying up or travelling – there have been cases of horses panicking in vehicles because this sort of headcollar has tightened and the horse has continued to fight against the pressure.

Halters are a cheap substitute for headcollars but have limited use. They should not be used for tying up and are not suitable for travelling because they are not as secure as a headcollar. Nor could you turn a horse out in one, as the leadrope is part of the headpiece and noseband. Strangely enough, white webbing halters are sometimes used for showing heavy horses in hand – their handlers must be very confident!

Halters are usually made of webbing or rope. The leadrope section goes under the horse's jaw and through a loop on the side of the noseband, where it is knotted to prevent it from slipping. This means it can neither pull tight on the horse's face nor slip loose. If it is fitted so that the noseband is slightly lower than that of an ordinary headcollar, you have a little more control.

## Lungeing

Lungeing and long reining are important steps in a young horse's education, and can also be useful to improve the way of going or solve problems with an older one. Lungeing is one of the first steps in teaching a horse to obey your voice, which can pay great dividends later on when you are trying to establish a communications system.

Traditionally, horses are lunged from a cavesson, which has a padded noseband with a choice of three rings on the front to which the lungeing rein is attached. A strap around the back of the jaw helps keep it in place; some cavessons have browbands, though they are not really necessary. If you use a browband, be careful how you introduce a young horse to the idea of having his ears touched by the cavesson.

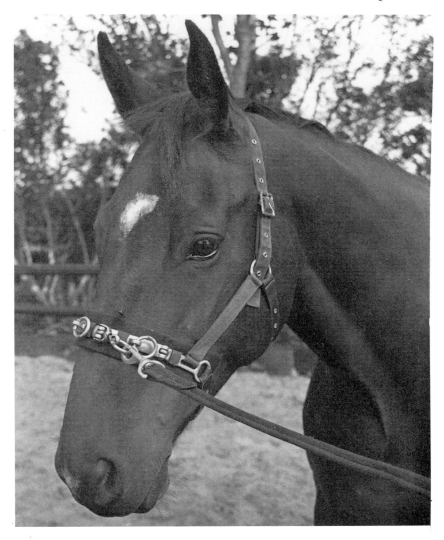

*A nylon lunge cavesson with padded noseband – not as nice as a leather one, but much cheaper.*

Most cavessons are fitted above the bit. The Wels cavesson, favoured by many Continental trainers, fastens below it and thus has an action similar to that of the drop noseband.

Unfortunately the lungeing cavesson falls down on one major design point. Until now, your young horse has been led by means of a leadrope attached to the back ring of a headcollar. Suddenly, you are expecting him to go forwards with a lungeing rein attached to the front of his nose – and as anything in front of the horse's face discourages forward movement, using a cavesson in this way does not make a lot of sense.

*In some circumstances and with some horses, you may be better off lungeing from a headcollar.*

Admittedly some horses take no notice at all of the lunge rein in front of their face. Others are irritated by it and may poke their noses up and out to get away from it, thus hollowing their backs and going in exactly the opposite way the trainer intended. Clipping the lunge rein to the front means that the cavesson has to be fastened perhaps more snugly than is comfortable – particularly for a young horse who is cutting teeth – to prevent the risk of it being pulled towards the horse's eye.

The above reasons mean that to introduce a young horse to lungeing, it is often better to fasten the lunge rein to the back ring of the cavesson, when it will not need to be fitted so tightly. Alternatively, use a well-fitting headcollar, again with the lunge rein fastened to the back ring. The headcollar should be fastened tighter than normal, but not so tight that it is uncomfortable. You will then be lungeing from a control point that the horse is used to.

Some people believe that it is not safe to lunge from a headcollar, but as lungeing should only be done in an enclosed area, how can it be any less safe than using a cavesson? If you have to lunge in the open or in potentially exciting circumstances – for instance, because you want to settle a young horse at a show before you get on him – you should lunge from the bit. If a horse decided to play up or take off on the end of the lunge, neither a cavesson nor a headcollar will leave you with much control!

Lunge reins are usually made from cotton webbing or nylon. The first is more expensive, but is nicer to handle: lightweight nylon lunge lines are useless as soon as there is the slightest amount of wind. Even if you wear gloves, which should be a golden rule when lungeing or long reining any horse, nylon can pull through your hands in a very uncomfortable way.

Lunge reins inevitably have a loop at the end. They would be a lot safer if they did not, because putting your hand through it is dangerous. If the horse plays up and the rein wraps round your hand, you could end up with a painful hand – or even worse, be dragged along the floor. The trouble is that even when you know you should not put your hand through the loop, the security it seems to offer can be tempting. It is too easy to use the loop without actually realising that you are doing it.

The lunge whip can be used to encourage the horse to move forwards or ask him to move out on the circle. Some are heavier than others, so choose one that is well balanced and you can handle easily. You can even buy telescopic lunge whips which break down into three sections – useful for storage or if you have to carry the whip in your car.

Lungeing from a cavesson or headcollar alone has limited use. It is necessary in the beginning to teach the horse what is required of him, but will not allow you to have much influence over his way of going. To work a horse on the lunge, as opposed to simply exercising him, he needs to wear a bit and either side reins, a Chambon or one of the other training aids discussed in Chapter 11.

He will also need to wear a bridle under the cavesson; if you use a headcollar, it must be one that adjusts on the nose as well as the headpiece. Take off the noseband, unless you want to use a drop one: a cavesson, Flash or Grakle will interfere. The cavesson or headcollar should be fitted so that the headpiece goes over the bridle headpiece, but the noseband goes inside the bridle cheekpieces. This means that there is no interference with the bit, but you will need to check that the fit is still correct: the extra bulk under the cheekpieces may necessitate letting the bit down a hole.

Side reins are designed to give the horse confidence in the bit and to enable the person on the ground to work him from behind, into the rein – just as you hope to do from the saddle. Some trainers use them on every horse, whilst others dislike them because they feel they are too fixed. Perhaps the best way is to accept that side reins, like most equipment, can be useful with some horses but not with others.

They seem most useful for the horse who is reluctant to take a contact, as here their static nature can be a bonus. Do not forget that the type of bit you use when lungeing is as important as when riding; here a bit which stays still in the mouth, such as an eggbutt or full-cheek snaffle, would make more sense than a loose-ring one.

Standard side reins are made from leather or nylon. Some incorporate elastic inserts or rubber rings designed to allow more 'give'; opinions vary as to which are best. One school of thought says that the reins which allow a little give are a closer approximation to the rider's hands, whereas the other believes that one-piece reins are more effective in teaching the horse that he will be more comfortable if he takes a steady contact. My vote goes to the former, as fixing your hands inevitably causes problems and fixing the reins might do the same.

As with any other piece of equipment, side reins are only useful if they are fitted correctly and the horse is lunged effectively. If they are too tight, they may make the horse tuck his nose in – but he will be restricted and his way of going will suffer. Similarly, if they are fitted too low, the horse is being forced into a shape rather than being worked in a way which encourages him to go forwards into a round outline.

Start off by fitting the side reins so that the horse takes a light contact when he is standing relaxed, with his nose in front of the vertical. As he gets used to them, shorten them gradually so that he works into a light contact when his nose is on or just in front of the vertical. What is important to remember is that he must work into a contact rather than the side reins pulling him into an outline.

If you are not sure how to lunge effectively, get someone who is to show you. Three or four minutes working on both reins, without side reins, will enable the horse to stretch himself and get his muscles working and you can then fit them as above.

Side reins should be fastened either to the girth straps of the saddle or to the rings on a roller. If using a saddle, fasten them at the top of the girth straps, not halfway down the horse's sides. Either remove the stirrups or – if the horse is to be ridden afterwards – run them up and wrap the leathers around the sides. The free end of the leather is then put through the loop thus made and finally through the keeper on the saddle flap. Now there is no risk of the irons slipping down and flapping against the horse.

Rollers need fitting with just as much care as saddles, since one which presses on the horse's back or withers can cause just as much damage. The top section should have a pad which goes either side of the spine, relieving any pressure on it. As an extra safeguard, you can use a foam pad underneath.

The most expensive breaking rollers are made from leather. If looked after well and kept soft and supple, these are good investments for anyone who intends to do a lot of breaking or lungeing. Economy webbing versions are more realistic for those who only have one horse. There is also a clever design which comprises the central section or back pad of the roller with straps on each side, and is used with an ordinary girth. This means that as long as you have a girth to fit, you can use the roller top on a horse or pony of any size.

Some trainers believe that you should not walk a horse with side reins, because they feel it shortens his stride, and there is an oft quoted piece of advice which says you should never lead a horse whilst he is wearing them. However, if they are fitted loose enough to allow him freedom of head and neck, there seems to be no reason why it

*Correctly fitted side reins give a light contact when the horse stands with his nose on or just in front of the vertical. Side reins which are too tight (see overleaf) encourage him to overbend and come behind the bit.*

would do him any harm – nor do they cause any problems when they are fitted for long reining, when the horse is walking for all or most of the time.

Riding with side reins cannot be recommended, because if the horse rears there is a danger that he could be unable to balance himself and fall over backwards. However, it has to be said that professional riders and trainers who know the risks and have the riding ability to match do sometimes ride with side reins fitted. They are usually fitted to horses who are being used for lunge lessons (for the rider's benefit, not the horse's) but horses chosen for this job should be steady and well behaved. Lunge lessons will also be held in an enclosed area.

Although standard side reins can be very useful for horses who are established in their way of going, some animals evade their action by leaning against them or coming above the bit. They also prevent the horse from stretching down and forwards (which is very different from leaning on the bit!). If this happens, running side reins, a Chambon

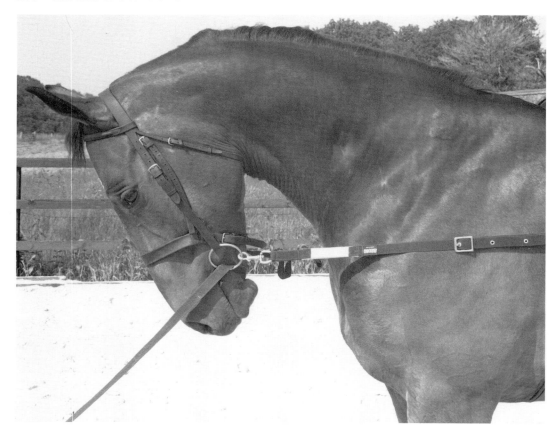

or one of the training aids that can be used for lungeing as well as riding (see Chapter 11) could be of more use.

Running side reins are similar in principle to ordinary running reins, but the main difference is that there is no rider and therefore no way they can be misused. An ineffectual or unaware rider can unfortunately use running reins to winch in the horse's head, but obviously this cannot happen on the lunge.

Running side reins start at the girth, like a martingale, then come between the forelegs and split into two. Each rein goes through the bit rings and fastens at the girth. It is a good idea to have buckle adjustments at the chest and the girth to give plenty of room for alteration and to avoid long loops at the girth.

The Chambon is very useful for the horse who goes in a hollow outline. Used correctly, it encourages him to stretch down and round and to lengthen the muscles along his back and topline that may have become cramped. One exception to this is the horse who is built 'long and low'; some Thoroughbreds are like this and will trot around quite happily with their noses nearly on the ground, without actually working the bits you are trying to influence!

*Lungeing in a Chambon encourages the horse to lower his head and neck and stretch his topline. This bridle has a drop noseband which adjusts on the nose as well as in the chin groove to give more leeway on fit. It was made specially for the author by Gibsons of Newmarket.*

On the Continent, trainers use the Chambon as a matter of course and regard it as standard lungeing equipment. Here, some people still tend to think of it as a gadget, with all that implies – which is a pity. However, it does seem that more people are realising how beneficial it can be. Event riders in particular find it useful for keeping horses loose and supple.

The Chambon is used in conjuction with a bridle and snaffle bit. It fastens to the girth and then splits into two lengths of cord or rolled leather, each with a small clip on the end. A short, padded strap with a ring at each end goes over the poll and fastens to the bridle headpiece. The cord or leather reins go through the rings on the end of the padded poll strap and down the sides of the horse's face, before clipping to the bit rings.

When you first introduce it, clip the rein ends directly to the poll strap rather than the bit rings. This gently introduces the idea that if the horse raises his head too high, he will feel pressure on his poll – and if he lowers his head, the pressure will be relieved.

There is no danger of him panicking or being overly stroppy, as might happen if you attached it to the bit straightaway.

As with any piece of equipment designed to influence the way the horse goes, it should be fitted fairly loosely until the horse is used to and is happy with its action. You can then adjust it gradually until it has the amount of influence you require.

The problem with books like this is that you cannot say that if you adjust a Chambon, side reins or whatever to X length for a horse who is X hands high you have the correct fitting. The best way of using any equipment you are not familiar with is to get someone who is familiar with it to help you. They can show you how to work the horse and adjust the tack so that the horse is comfortable and happy.

The Chambon has been included in this chapter rather than the one on training aids because it should be used only for lungeing, not for riding.

## Long reining

Long reining is an excellent way of teaching a young horse to stop, start, turn and accept the actions of a bit without the impediment of a rider. It teaches him how to go forwards and straight and can also be used to help overcome some cases of nappiness. Horses who are reluctant to go out alone or in front of another horse often benefit from being taught to long rein; once they accept the idea of being driven forwards, they seem to gain confidence. If the horse who is reluctant to hack out alone is first long reined round quiet routes, he often relaxes and continues to behave under saddle.

The good news from a financial viewpoint is that if you have already been lungeing your horse, all you need to buy to long rein is a second lunge rein. These clip to the bit rings – or to the side rings of a cavesson if you want to introduce him to the experience this way.

Some trainers like to first introduce the horse to long reining by lungeing him on a circle with two reins. If you have the skill, you can lunge very effectively by this method because you have an inside rein and an outside one. You also have two handfuls of lunge reins and need to be careful not to let the outside one slip down over the horse's hocks and get clamped under his tail – it takes practice, and as with every other skill, your first 'victim' should be an experienced horse, not a youngster.

If you are long reining, as opposed to lungeing with two reins, it is safest to put a saddle on the horse, run down the irons on shortened leathers and pass the reins through the irons. This helps to keep the long reins out of harm's way as much as possible. As an extra precaution, you can fasten the irons to the girth to prevent them from flapping around.

Unless you have a particular reason for not doing so, it is also a good idea to fit the horse with side reins. These should be loosely adjusted but they do help you to stay in control. When you are walking behind and slightly to one side of the horse, there is a lot of rein between you and the bit.

*Two lunge lines of equal weight are used for long reining. Correctly fitted side reins give extra control.*

When long reining, as when lungeing, you should wear gloves. If you do have to drop one rein and grab the other with both hands to keep your horse under control (which never happens in 'how-to' scenarios but unfortunately can happen in real life) you are less likely to have the skin taken off your palms.

To lunge 'by the book' you should wear a hard hat to give some protection from flying hooves if the horse dives in and cuts past you, though many people would argue that this is not always necessary. However, it is a sensible precaution when long reining – if the horse kicks out, which can happen if he does not want to go forward, you might find yourself in a vulnerable position.

## Protective boots and bandages

Work boots and bandages are yet another area of controversy. Some people use them all the time, even when their horses are turned out. Others take the opposite view and maintain that they make tendons and ligaments lazy and the horse less careful.

There is a middle course to be steered through the arguments. It makes sense to protect a horse who is unbalanced (such as a youngster) or who moves badly, or who is doing high-risk work such as galloping or jumping. But to put them on a horse who is turned out, or is taking part in long rides over varied terrain, has its drawbacks: sweaty skin becomes soft and susceptible to infection and dirt trapped between boot and leg can set up similar problems.

There are many designs of boot and many kinds of material, including some with high-impact resistance from the automotive and ballistics industries. The horse who has everything can now have bullet-proof boots!

But before spending a fortune on a set of high-tech, stylish boots with fancy patterns and fancy fastenings, decide what job you need them to do. Look at styles in all price ranges; the most expensive are not always the best. A beautifully designed set of Continental boots lies barely used in my tack collection; the boots themselves are shaped and padded to perfection, but one or other of the clever-looking securing straps with clip fastenings always seems to come undone no matter how carefully the boots are put on.

At one time strap and buckle fastenings were the rule, and still give the best security in some cases. The downside is that they are sometimes fiddly to put on, especially when you are short of time and your fingers are cold. In those situations, quick and easy fastenings such as Velcro save time and patience – as long as you remember to accustom the horse to the noise of them opening and closing before you use them, and to keep the Velcro free of bits of bedding, etc that would lessen its 'stickability'.

Boots and bandages are only worth buying and using if they protect the leg against the impact of a shod foot. Some boots are so flimsy that they offer no more than a token gesture towards protection, yet they can still be expensive.

They must also be kept clean. If you have to use them when, for instance, you are riding or lungeing the horse in a sand school, grains of sand are inevitably going to get trapped between the boot and the horse's leg. The boots must be cleaned thoroughly before they are used again, or you will be rubbing sand into skin – try it on yourself and see how uncomfortable it is.

As with other tack, boots and bandages must be put on and adjusted correctly. If you place boots designed to protect the leg slightly higher than you want them to finish up, then gently slide them down into place, you will ensure that the hair underneath lies flat. Fasten them tight enough to stay in place but not so tight that they are going to pinch or rub.

The best way of fastening four- or five-strap boots is to hold the boot in place with one hand and secure the third strap with the other. This should stop the boot slipping down or flapping about while you fasten the others. On styles that start just below the knee, you will often find the top strap needs to be slightly tighter than the bottom one if the boot is not to interfere with the movement of the fetlock joint.

Listed below are the main types of leg protection you are likely to come across or want to use. They are all meant to be used when the horse is working; leg protection for travelling is dealt with in the next chapter. They should not be used as a substitute for veterinary advice or the skills of a good farrier: if your horse habitually knocks himself, or stumbles, ask your vet to check him.

*Brushing boots* are designed, not surprisingly, for horses who brush (knock the inside of one leg with the opposite hoof). Many people use them as standard, especially on young horses, but some designs are made from materials so flimsy they are of very little value. They should have a strike pad down the inside of the leg so that the vulnerable area has extra protection and be fastened so that the long strap ends point backwards – this means that there is no danger of the horse knocking one boot against the other and pulling one of them off.

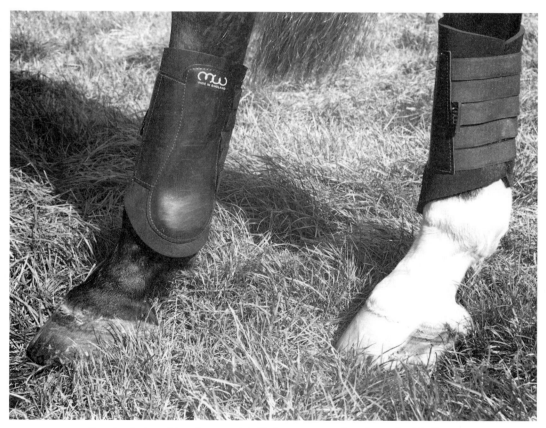

*Synthetic brushing boots with Velcro straps, fitted on the hindlegs.*

*Ring boots are used on horses who move too close behind. Usually only one is worn; this horse, who also has leather fetlock boots with strap and buckle fastenings, moves particularly close.*

*Ring boots* are also designed to protect the horse who knocks one leg with the opposite one. Only one is worn, and it is usually fitted to the vulnerable leg rather than the one which causes the damage. It comprises a hollow ring made from thick, tough rubber. A strap runs through the centre and is used to fasten it round the pastern. Sometimes it works quite well, but it is usually not as safe or effective as a good pair of brushing or speedicut boots.

*Speedicut boots* are longer versions of brushing boots to give extra protection to the inside top of the cannon bone and the inside of the fetlock. It is possible to buy brushing and speedicut boots which extend over the back of the fetlock as well as covering the inside of it. Like brushing boots, you will find that hind boots are made slightly longer than front ones; this is because the front cannon bones are usually shorter than the hind ones. However, if your horse has longer than usual front cannons there is nothing to stop you using hind boots on them.

*Fetlock boots* protect the horse's equivalent of our ankle. If you are going to use these, you might as well use brushing boots which protect the cannon bone as well.

*Synthetic fetlock boots with Velcro fastenings.*

*Polo boots* are like brushing boots, but extend down the pastern and over the coronet. Obviously designed for polo ponies, who turn at speed and whose legs are at risk from balls, sticks and other ponies, they can also be used for less risky activities.

*Tendon boots* do not, as many people believe, give any form of support to the tendons. They are purely for protection – the strike pad down the back of the leg means that if the horse hits the back of a front leg with a hind hoof, as can happen when galloping or jumping, the boot should stop him slicing into a tendon. You can choose from either closed- or open-fronted styles. Showjumpers tend to favour open-fronted tendon boots, as they feel these protect the tendons but do not encourage the horse to be careless. The theory is that if he hits a pole, he will be encouraged to pick his feet up higher next time.

*German made tendon boots with strap and clip fastenings and rubber overreach boots with Velcro fastenings.*

There is an American boot, also available in this country and called Professional's Choice, which is claimed to support tendons and ligaments. It has a suspensory strap designed to act like a sling which is said to have helped many animals whose legs have been weakened through injury.

*Yorkshire boots* are the simplest of all, but can be surprisingly effective where the interference of one leg with another is only mild. Often only one is worn; the boot is simply a rectangle of thick felt with a tape sewn along its length, just below the centre. The boot is placed on the leg so that the tape is on the outside and the largest rectangle

*Open-fronted tendon boots protect the vulnerable tendon area but discourage the horse from being blasé about hitting poles in front.*

of felt is above it. The tape is tied just tight enough to keep the boot in place and the top half of the felt folded down over it giving two layers of fabric for protection.

*Overreach boots* are bell-shaped and fit over the coronet and heel. The idea is that they protect the horse if he overreaches – strikes into the back of a front foot with the front of a back one. Overreach injuries can be deep and hard to heal, as they often open and close every time the horse moves.

The original overreach boots were simply one-piece rubber bells. Some people still use them because they are cheaper than other designs and there are no fastenings to come undone; their disadvantage is that they are not the easiest things to put on and take off.

*Yorkshire boots are simple, but often surprisingly effective.*

To put one on, first turn it inside out. Hold the horse's front hoof against your knees like a farrier does – easier said than done with some animals – and pull the boot over the hoof. Once it is in place, turn it the right way out.

Overreach boots with strap or Velcro fastenings are more expensive but save a lot of time, effort and broken fingernails. Whether you use these or the ones with fasteners, make sure they are not so long that the horse is likely to stand on one and trip himself up. Sometimes it is safer to trim the edges with scissors.

Leaf pattern or petal overreach boots, which have rows of separate 'petals' attached to a strap which fastens around the pastern, avoid the risk of the horse tripping. If he stands on the boot, the petal pulls off and can be replaced with another. They do not turn inside out, which can sometimes happen with the rubber kind. The trouble with these boots is that they flap, very noisily – something the horse may have to get used to and you will have to put up with!

*Coronet boots* protect the horse from tread injuries in that vulnerable area. If this is a risk, you are usually better off using overreach boots, which protect a larger area. You might get a few funny looks if you use them on the horse's hindlegs – some horse people are not very good at lateral thinking – but if they work, does it matter?

*Knee boots* come in two designs, one for travelling and the other for exercise. The exercise version is often called a skeleton knee boot, as it has a round central pad to cover the front of the knee, but open sides. The reasoning behind them is that if a horse comes down on the road, they protect the knee from injury, but some designs can be more trouble than they are worth.

They have to be fastened so that the top strap is tight enough to keep them in place but not so tight that it restricts the leg. The bottom strap should be very loose; its purpose is merely to stop the knee pad flapping about, not to keep the boot in place.

They are unsuitable for anything but slow work – and no matter how carefully you fit them, some designs are prone to slipping; those with Velcro fastenings are the worst offenders. If a boot slips down, the rider is unlikely to notice until the horse stands on it and trips – which could lead to the sort of injury it was supposed to prevent in the first place!

*Exercise bandages* are used to protect the legs from knocks; it used to be thought that they could provide support to tendons and ligaments, but many vets now believe that it is unlikely they can do this. They should *always* be used over padding and should only be used by those who have been taught how to put them on correctly.

They start just below the knee and usually finish just above the fetlock, so there is no interference with joints. The turns must be even to give equal tension, and made towards the horse's tail. If tie tapes are used, they should be fastened no tighter than the bandage turns. The knot should be on the outside or the leg, not on the back, where it could press on a tendon, or at the front, where it would press on the cannon bone.

If you use bandages with Velcro fastenings, they should finish so that the tapes are on the outside of the legs with the ends facing towards the horse's tail. If the ends face forwards and the horse brushes one leg against the other, they could be pulled undone.

Some riders like to tape over bandage fastenings or sew them for extra security. Sewing is safest: if you use tape, it must not be any tighter than the bandage turns or you will be applying unwanted pressure.

One of the country's leading veterinary surgeons, who specialises in competition horses, says the injuries he has seen have convinced him that bandages and padding will not protect a galloping or jumping horse from slicing into his tendon. For work of this kind he recommends well-designed tendon boots with a back-strike pad.

It is also possible to buy impact-resistant leg protector pads which fit over the tendon area and are bandaged in place.

# Chapter 10
# Rugs and Travelling Equipment

There are so many types of rug available that it would be easy for the well-dressed horse to have a wardrobe larger than that of his owners. Fortunately, modern fabrics mean that many rugs can do more than one job – and they are also a lot easier to handle and look after than old-fashioned ones such as those made from jute.

The amount of rugs you need depends on your horse's type, the way you keep him and the work he is doing. For instance, whilst a clipped horse will need outdoor and indoor rugs to keep him warm and dry, native ponies often manage best with the coats nature gave them, provided they have adequate shelter.

There are four main types of clothing: New Zealand or turnout rugs and stable rugs form the basic requirements, with anti-sweat rugs and lightweight summer sheets as useful extras. If you travel your horse in a horsebox or trailer, he will need rugs suitable for the weather and the vehicle – which could mean a rug or combination of rugs from his standard wardrobe or clothing kept specifically for that purpose.

Multi-purpose rugs which can be used in the stable, when travelling or as anti-sweat rugs are particularly useful. Some owners may also find that they need exercise rugs to keep the back and loins of a clipped horse warm on slow winter exercise.

The quality and prices of rugs vary enormously, from cheap and cheerful to hundreds of pounds. In general – though not always – you get what you pay for. The more expensive rugs are usually better cut; their prices reflect the materials used and the time and skill that goes into making them.

## Fit and design

A rug only works if it fits properly and stays in place. That might sound obvious, but a lot of rugs fail on two counts. One is that they are not cut properly to begin with, and the other – which is not the manufacturers' fault – is that people buy the wrong size.

To work out what size rug your horse needs, first take the measurement A to B, from the centre of the chest to the quarters. This gives the basic length needed: standard rugs are made in three-inch increments. It also helps to measure from C to D, from just in front of the withers to the top of the tail, and from C to A, from just in front of the withers, down the side of the neck to the centre of the chest. These measurements, together with a description of your horse's type (eg Thoroughbred, cob, middleweight half-bred) should enable a good retailer to advise you what size and make of rug would suit him best.

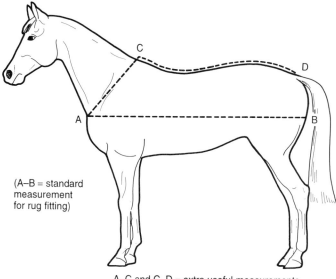

(A–B = standard measurement for rug fitting)

A–C and C–D = extra useful measurements

Rugs, like clothes, come in standard sizes. Horses, like people, are not always standard shapes. Some are long in the back, some are straight in the shoulder, some are wide across the chest and quarters and so on. Rugs, like off-the-peg clothes, are tailored to an average set of proportions.

If your horse's conformation means you cannot find a ready-made rug that gives a good fit, many good companies will combine pattern parts from different sizes to make one that will. This will add about 10 per cent to the standard price, though a few 'upmarket' companies will make to measure at no extra cost.

Some people buy a size or even two sizes larger than their horse actually needs because they think that the farther it comes down over the top of the tail, the warmer he will be. Usually what happens is the rug slips back or to the side and the horse ends up sore or uncomfortable. White hairs on the withers are more often a sign of a badly fitting rug than a badly fitting saddle.

Good fit goes hand in hand with good design. According to the best manufacturers – and there is a handful whose rugs always seem to stay in place no matter what the wearer does – the most important area in terms of cutting a rug is the neck. It needs to be fairly high; if the rug gapes, it will slip back and put pressure on the withers and possibly the spine.

A snug but not restricting fit around the neck should be coupled with correct shaping in the shoulders, so that the rug does not pull tight when the horse moves. This is achieved through a combination of cut and darting; outdoor rugs, which hopefully stay in place when the horse gallops, rolls and does any of the other energetic things which horses tend to do in fields, sometimes have a pleat in each side at the front to give extra leeway.

The quarters must also be shaped and darted so that the rug conforms to the contours of the horse. Cheaper rugs, particularly New Zealands, sometimes do not have darts, and consequently do not mould to the horse – so wind and rain blow underneath. The only exceptions to this rule are rugs made from knitted fabrics, which – as long as the overall cut is good – mould to the horse's shape without darting.

## Fittings

Rugs fasten at the chest and are held in place by various systems of fastenings. The only one to avoid at all costs is the old-fashioned surcingle, which is simply a wide belt that goes over the horse's back, round his belly and fastens on the side. This puts pressure on the spine and can lead to back problems.

Some people still use rollers, similar in design to those used for breaking but without the metal rings to attach side reins. Unless they are well designed and fitted with the greatest care, they can also cause pressure problems. They should be designed to clear the withers and spine, but most people who use them add a foam pad underneath for extra protection. If your horse has high withers, you will find it hard to get a roller with sufficient clearance.

Anti-cast rollers are supposed to be a safety measure for horses who get cast – lie down or roll in their stables and trap themselves against the wall when they try to get up again. These are made with a metal arch over the spine, set into just the right place to dig into and bruise the horse if he rolls!

The commonest rug fastenings are cross surcingles and hind legstraps; front legstraps are not seen so often. The best system of all is arguably the Pape's pattern harness and similar designs which go from the chest, between the horse's front legs and under his belly to fasten on to the sides of the rug.

These 'spider pattern' harnesses, which look complicated but are actually very easy to adjust and use, keep the rug in place without any danger of putting pressure on the withers or spine. Read the manufacturers' instructions, as their operation may vary slightly from one company to another.

When you put a rug on, fold the back to the front and place it over his shoulders, in front of the withers, farther forward than you want it to end up. This ensures that when you slide it back into place, the horse's coat will lie flat underneath. If the hair is pushed the wrong way, the horse will be uncomfortable and may bite or chew at his rug to try and relieve the irritation.

Do up the front fastening, then unfold it along his back. Cross surcingles should be fastened so that they cross in the centre of his belly, and adjusted so that you can fit a

*Outdoor rugs should stay in place whatever the horse does!*

hand's width between each surcingle and the horse. Elasticated ones which 'give' as he breathes must be more comfortable than plain webbing.

Hind legstraps are usually linked and are fastened so that each is clipped to the side from which it originates. In other words, first pass the left legstrap behind the nearside hindleg and fasten it to the back of the rug, also on the left. Then pass the right legstrap round the offside hindleg, link it through the left hand one and fasten it to the back of the rug at the right hand side. You should again be able to get a hand's width between the legstraps and the horse.

If the horse is wearing a rug with legstraps for the first time, take extra care. He may kick out at the unaccustomed feel, so be careful while you fasten them. Walk him round the stable so he gets used to the feel of the straps before you take him outside: trying to hang on to a youngster who has been startled by the feel of the legstraps on his new turnout rug is not easy!

Lightweight rugs often have fillet strings or straps at the back to prevent the rug blowing up in the wind. If you have ever seen a fit, clipped horse explode when his

*This Rambo rug by Horseware is particularly well shaped – note the close but not restricting fit round the neck – and incorporates a tail flap. It is waterproof and breathable.*

exercise rug is lifted by a sudden blow, you will understand why this can be a very good idea! They go under the horse's tail and should be no tighter than is necessary to help keep the rug in place.

When you remove a rug, undo the legstraps first (if fitted) and clip them to the sides of the rug out of harm's way. Then undo the front of the rug and finally the cross surcingles, if fitted. The reason for doing things in this order is that if the horse moves when the surcingles are undone, you will not be struggling to cope with a rug that is dangling between the front legs of a possibly frightened animal.

The quality of rug fittings varies as widely as that of the rugs themselves. The nicest of all are brass, which do not rust or seize up like cheaper kinds. Plastic fittings work until they break – which in some cases is all too soon. Cheaper metal fastenings go rusty in time.

## Outdoor rugs
Outdoor rugs range from the toughest New Zealands, designed to take on any weather, to paddock rugs meant for much lighter use – perhaps on a stabled horse turned out for

short periods in not too severe weather. It is not fair to buy a paddock rug and then complain when it does not protect a horse living out all the time, so before you buy, check what the rug is meant to do.

One or two manufacturers are brave enough to claim that their rugs are totally waterproof. Most claim that their toughest designs give as much protection as can reasonably be expected; the British Equestrian Trade Association, which represents many manufacturers and retailers, says that the most you should realistically expect from a rug is that it keeps the worst of the weather off your horse.

Rugs have stitching, seams and fastenings, so it would be very difficult to make one that never allowed any water in when worn for most of the time. You should always have two outdoor rugs, so that if one is subjected to a long period of heavy rain, or gets damaged, you have a spare while it is dried off or repaired.

Damage is another complaint frequently made by owners. It is actually an unfair one because if a rug did not have a breaking point the horse would be at risk. If he managed to get himself caught up on something – and horses have the knack of doing this, even in the safest seeming surroundings – which would you rather broke first, the rug or his leg?

Similarly, while there are many tough fabrics available, it would be impossible to make something that could stand up to another horse's teeth or to barbed wire. Barbed wire is potentially lethal and should never be used to fence in horses, but some people seem happy to take the risk.

New Zealand rugs were traditionally made from canvas, which only reaches peak efficiency when it has been wet and dried naturally two or three times. This is because the fibres swell, making it harder for water to penetrate – either use it in light rain for the first few times or simulate your own showers with a hosepipe. It needs re-proofing occasionally – how often depends on how much it is used. There are several good re-proofing products available from most saddlers, designed to be painted on with a large paintbrush or sprayed on.

The vulnerable areas on any outdoor rug are those with stitching and seams. To keep the horse comfortable, the fabric also needs to 'breathe' to a certain extent; if there is not a passage of air in and out, the horse will get hot and sweaty underneath. Traditional fabrics which allow for this will eventually become waterlogged if they are not allowed to dry after heavy rain.

Over the past few years there have been some excellent rugs developed in high-tech, lightweight fabrics that have both waterproof and breathable properties. They are much easier to handle and care for than traditional canvas, which becomes heavy when wet. It is important to remember that when a rug is lightweight, it must be particularly well-designed to be suitable for outdoor use.

When the weather is bad, a horse will stand so that he has his back to the wind and rain. If his lightweight rug does not have the right cut and fastenings to keep it in place, it will lift off his back and the wind and rain will go underneath, leaving you with a dry rug but a wet horse.

Tail flaps and neck covers give extra protection. Neck covers, which fasten to the top and front of the rug, help to retain a surprising amount of body heat. They have the added advantage of keeping more of the horse clean; trying to get mud out of a mane usually means that you end up dirtier than the horse.

You can also buy hoods that cover the neck and head and have holes for ears and eyes. Some people like them, while others feel there is a risk, even with the best designed styles, that the hood could slip and cover one or both of the horse's eyes.

Hoods made from lightweight stretch fabric are said to help some horses who suffer from sweet itch. This is an allergy to a type of biting midge which results in itchiness and rubbing, and animals who are badly affected will rub their manes and tails raw. These hoods can also be used to train unruly manes to lie flat.

## Stable rugs, summer sheets and anti-sweat rugs

Stable rugs are used to give extra warmth while the horse is stabled. A well-designed stable will have good ventilation but no draughts; do not make the mistake of thinking that you can keep your horse warmer by shutting the top door because that only creates an unhealthy environment. He will be breathing stale air, contaminated by ammonia, etc from urine and droppings, which will worsen and in some cases cause respiratory problems. If you want to add more warmth, use an extra or a different rug.

At one time horses used to wear smart woollen day rugs during the daytime, when they were less likely to lie down and soil them, and jute night rugs. Modern fabrics have made jute rugs superfluous and woollen rugs are kept for travelling and times when the horse is on display – they often have the owner's initials or the sponsor's name or logo in one corner.

The commonest rugs are those with a quilted nylon outer and a cotton lining. Although they are often sold as 'machine washable', many of the bulkier ones will not fit into an ordinary washing machine. If you have a big horse and a thick quilted rug, you will definitely have to find a launderette with a large machine.

New fabrics have enabled some manufacturers to cut down on bulk but provide even more warmth than many quilted rugs. Two good examples are rugs made from thermal, knitted fabrics and those which incorporate Flectalon.

The thermal knit fabrics mould to the horse's shape, so they are a good choice for animals whose conformation makes fitting rugs a problem. They have special wicking properties which means that moisture is transferred from the horse through to the outside of the rug – this makes them useful for drying off a sweating horse or one that has been bathed or swum. Because they do not have the bulk of ordinary quilted rugs, even the largest sizes can be washed in an ordinary machine.

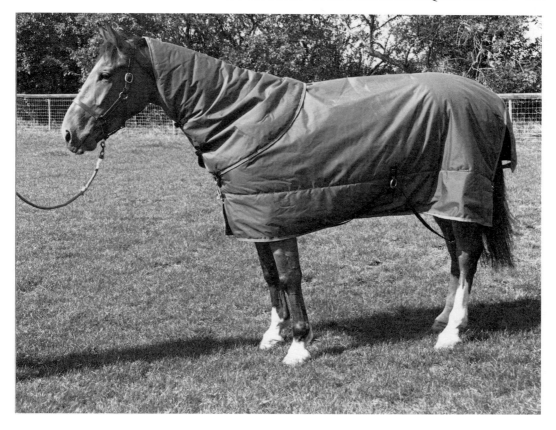

*A made-to-measure New Zealand rug and neck cover by Rees Tack.*

Flectalon is a lightweight material which has good insulating properties and also reflects the horse's own body heat. It was first used in astronauts' suits and survival blankets. The company which uses it makes rugs in two weights, and claims that the one for the most severe conditions will keep the wearer warm at temperatures down to minus 20 degrees Centigrade.

Cotton summer sheets – they are called sheets rather than rugs because the fabric is so thin and light – are used to keep draughts off the horse when travelling in warm weather and to protect thin-skinned animals from flies. Some grey and coloured horses who suffer from photosensitisation problems may even need to wear a lightweight cotton sheet when turned out in hot weather. If so, use one with cross surcingles that should stay in place – and do not expect it to last forever. If horses can destroy tough New Zealands, think how much easier a cotton sheet will be!

If you use a cotton sheet under a heavier stable rug, it will help keep your horse clean and cut down on trips to the launderette with the top rug. The cotton sheet can be washed as often as necessary, so the horse has a clean layer of fabric next to his skin.

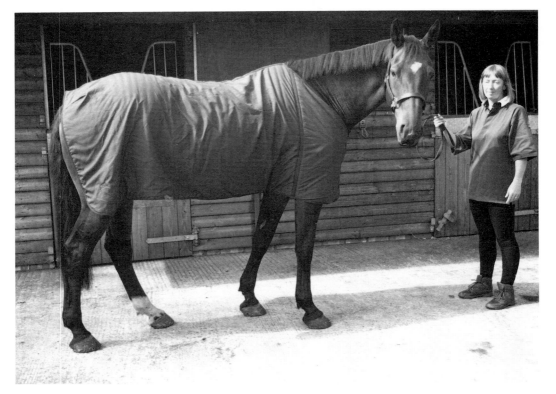

*This Thermatex stable rug is one of the latest designs. Beautifully cut, it stays in place with just an under-belly fastening and – like the other rugs pictured – does not put pressure on the withers or spine. Warm, lightweight and breathable, it has a thermal inner and a tough outer which does not pick up shavings or other bedding materials (see opposite). It will also fit in an ordinary washing machine.*

Traditional anti-sweat rugs, which work on the same principle as men's string vests, are not as popular as they used to be. Multi-purpose lightweight thermal rugs and 'coolers' made from high-tech, close-mesh fabrics are more useful for most people and keep their shape better; string rugs stretch and tear easily.

However, they can still do the job they are designed for as long as they are used correctly, with another lightweight rug or cotton sheet on top. You need two rugs to trap a layer of air, thus helping to dry off the horse. Many people use mesh anti-sweat rugs on their own, which is a waste of time.

## Rug care and maintenance

Dirty rugs can cause skin problems. Machine-washable rugs are the easiest to look after, but you need to be careful about the cleaning agent you use. Avoid 'biological'

washing powders and any with 'brighteners' or strong perfumes, as these can set up an allergic reaction. The same applies to washing numnahs and bandages.

If you are not sure whether a rug can be washed, check with the retailer or manufacturer. Do not exceed recommended temperatures even if they seem conservative; if you use water that is too hot, you may shrink either the lining or the outer fabric and end up with a distorted rug.

Heavy New Zealands should have dried mud brushed off regularly. You should also brush the hair off the lining – as with stable rugs, using a cotton sheet underneath helps to keep the horse clean.

Scrubbing New Zealand rugs is hard, dirty and unpleasant work. A power washer – one of the smaller sort sold in DIY stores for washing cars and other jobs – makes life much easier. Leather legstraps and chest fastenings will need treating with oil or leather food and clip fastenings may need a drop of oil to keep them opening and closing smoothly.

If a rug needs mending, make sure it is as clean as possible before asking a saddler to carry out repairs. Most will refuse to handle equipment unless it is clean and dry – understandably so, as not only is it unpleasant to handle, but it damages sewing machines.

Check rugs before they are stored and only put them away if they are clean and dry. Do not store them anywhere damp, or they will develop mould – and remember that moths, mice and rats like nothing better than nice cosy rugs. I once kept a horse on a livery yard where someone had left a New Zealand rug hanging up for several weeks without checking it: when she took it down, a large rat leapt out of the corner of the lining, where it had made a nest!

## Travelling equipment

There are two schools of thought on travelling equipment. One says that all the vulnerable areas – poll, legs and dock – should be covered. The other, less traditional, view is that if the vehicle is well padded, the horse is better off travelling without extra clothing.

Continental transporters usually travel horses on long journeys without leg or tail protection, and seem to have no more problems than traditionalists who wrap them up in the proverbial cotton wool. There is also a theory that if a horse's legs are wrapped up in layers of bandage and padding, he is more likely to become hot and irritated and start stamping about, thus increasing the risk of injury.

So who is right? Certainly it is impractical to put travelling gear on foals, who travel loose with their mothers, but most people feel happier if their horses have some protection. The ground rules are that you should only use equipment that is going to do some good, and you must be able to put it on properly.

It is always best to travel a horse in either a leather headcollar or one with rings that are designed to break easily. Nylon headcollars are too strong for this purpose: if they get caught up and the horse panics, he could do a lot of damage to himself. You should always tie your headcollar rope to a piece of string, not directly to a metal ring. This extra breaking point does not make it safe to use an ordinary nylon headcollar – if the headcollar itself should get caught up, the breakable tying up loop will not help. Be careful that your loop will actually break if needs be – some types of baler twine are too strong for this purpose.

There are some cleverly designed ropes on the market which incorporate safety clips at the headcollar end. If the horse pulls back too hard, the clip opens and the rope falls away. The problem with the loop of string method is that if the horse pulls back and breaks away, he is left with a length of rope dangling round his legs.

Very big horses, or those who are prone to tossing their heads about, are safer if they have the extra protection of a pollguard. This is usually a padded cap with slits for the headcollar to pass through and earholes; make sure the earholes are big enough, as anything which pinches the base of the ears will irritate the horse and make him throw his head around even more. If necessary, enlarge them with scissors.

The rugs you use will depend on the weather when you leave home – and the forecaster's predictions. It is always better to take rugs you do not use than to find you have arrived with a cold horse. Remember that if your horse has worked hard, his muscles will have done the same. If he is tired and has exerted himself he must be kept warm and dry – this is where thermal rugs which wick moisture through and keep the horse comfortable underneath are so useful.

Tail bandages and tailguards have two uses. One is to provide the tail bones with extra padding, which will give protection if the horse sits back while he is travelling, and the other is to keep a pulled tail in shape. Tail bandages are made from stretch fabric and – as with leg bandages – need to be used with care.

They must not be used for long periods, or there is a danger that they will restrict the circulation. This can lead to sores under the dock, hair follicles being destroyed so that the hair grows back white, and even worse injuries. The bandages must also be put on so that the pressure is even and not too tight.

Bandages must be rolled the right way before being applied. To do this pick up the pointed end, which will have tapes or a Velcro strip sewn into it, and lay the fastenings down the inside. Fold over the end and start rolling so that the tapes are on the inside.

To put on a tail bandage, dampen the hair slightly. Never wet the tail bandage, or it will tighten as it dries and cause circulation problems. Slide the bandage underneath the top of the dock, leaving a few inches which are folded down over the first turn or two – this is then bandaged over, which helps to keep everything secure. The turns should keep the same tension, tight enough not to slip but not so tight that they could cause discomfort.

Bandage down to just below the tail bones, then take the turns back up again. Tie the tapes in a double knot on the outside centre of the tail, keeping their tension the same as the bandage's, and if possible pull down one turn of fabric to cover them. Finish by bending the tail gently back into position.

To remove a tail bandage, undo the tapes and grasp the tail bandage at the top. You should be able to slide it off with one movement. If your horse's tail has been plaited, you will need to unwrap the bandage rather than pulling it off to keep your handiwork in place.

All this presupposes that your horse is one of the co-operative ones. Most do not mind having tail bandages put on, but some hate it and clamp their tails down so tightly that getting a bandage on is a battle of wills. Rather than have a fight, you could opt instead for a padded tailguard; some of the best designs have Velcro fastenings and do not need to be attached to a roller. Traditional tailguards fasten round the dock with tapes or Velcro and have long tapes at the top which attach to a roller.

If you need to keep your horse's tail spotlessly clean on the way to a show – particularly if he is grey – use a leg from an old pair of tights or stockings as a 'tail bag' and bandage over the top. An alternative but more time consuming method is to use a second tail bandage below the first one.

Whether you use bandages or boots on your horse's legs is down to personal preference, as each has advantages and disadvantages. Bandages take longer to put on and take off, though with practice the time factor gets shorter, but are less likely to slip. Boots are quick and easy, but only the shaped and usually more expensive ones stay in place well. Cheap boots – usually padded rectangles with Velcro fastenings – are often unwieldy and do not stay in place.

Many people do not use bandages either because they are worried about putting them on too tight or because they find them too fiddly to take off an excited horse. When a four-year-old arrives at its first show with eyes on stalks, the last thing you want is to have to dodge flying hooves whilst you unravel bandages. The answer to the first problem is that if you get someone experienced to show you how to put them on, and watch whilst you practise, you will soon learn the technique. As they are always used over thick padding, it is unlikely that they could be fastened tight enough to cause any damage.

You can also use bandages to your advantage in solving the second problem. If you tape over the fastenings, making sure that your tape is no tighter than the bandage turns so there is no uneven pressure, you can leave the bandages on whilst you work in. They will protect your horse's legs while he bounces around in excitement and you can leave them on until he settles down. Once his brain is back between his ears, you can take them off in safety.

Travelling and stable bandages are made from the same fabrics and are interchangeable. (Stable bandages, also used over padding, provide warmth and perhaps a little support for a tired, cold or sick horse.) The easiest to use are those made from stretch jersey, as they mould better to the horse's leg.

Ideally, these bandages should be long enough to enable you to start bandaging just below the knee, carry down to just below the fetlock and go back up the leg. Unfortunately many manufacturers do not make them long enough to do this on big horses with plenty of bone, in which case you either have to find another make or start bandaging lower down. Admittedly it is the padding rather than the bandage that gives the protection, but two full layers keep it in place better.

The two commonest types of padding are Gamgee and Fybagee. Gamgee is cotton wool sandwiched between gauze layers, and is excellent for veterinary purposes. The problem with using it for travelling is that you cannot wash it, so it works out very expensive. Fybagee, which is a sort of felt, can be washed and re-used time after time. You can also buy quilted cotton bandage pads, which do not act as a magnet for shavings and straw in the way that Fybagee seems to.

Putting on travelling bandages may be easy to describe but takes practice to get right. For a start, you have to develop the knack of holding the padding in place while you bandage; using shaped padding, which covers the knees and hocks, gives extra protection. As with other bandages, the turns should be even so there are no pressure points.

Bandage so that your turns are made towards the horse's tail. When you finish, tie the tapes on the outside of the leg. If they are tied on the inside they could come undone, whilst if they are on the back or the front of the leg they will press on the tendon and cannon bone respectively. Velcro tapes should finish in the same position, with the ends of the tapes pointing towards the horse's tail so they do not catch on the opposite leg and pull undone.

The coronet band will be less vulnerable to injury if your padding covers it: some horses have an amazing knack of standing on themselves. Overreach boots front *and* back protect both the coronet band and the heel and also minimise the risk of the horse pulling off a front shoe by standing on the heels.

The old grooms used Sandown bandages, but for some reason these are now hard to find – or perhaps it is just that they are more fiddly to make and manufacturers do not want the bother. The Sandown bandage has a padded and a non-padded end, so does not need extra padding underneath; you start with the padded end next to the leg, then

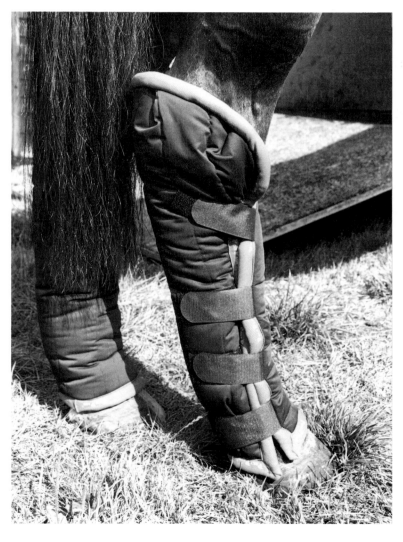

*Travelling boots must be well shaped if they are not to slip. These boots, by PI Associates, are a particularly good example.*

*Bandages should only be used over padding. Under-bandage wraps such as these Rappas are becoming as popular as traditional Gamgee and Fybagee*

continue down and up again as before so the non-padded section keeps the whole thing in place.

Some people like to use knee and hock boots for travelling. They are useful for horses which kick or paw the ground and bang their knees on the vehicle, but have to be fastened so that the top straps are tight enough to keep them in place. The bottom straps are fastened very loosely so as not to interfere with the joint. However, they can rub or pinch thin-skinned horses.

# Chapter 11
## Training Aids

In an ideal world, every horse would work beautifully in a simple snaffle or double bridle, with no need for martingales, draw reins, balancing reins or any other gadgets. Unfortunately, the real world does not work like that; horses develop problems in their way of going and riders cannot always solve them without extra help. Most of the problems are, admittedly, caused by riders rather than the horses themselves – but that does not always help the person who is trying to solve them, especially if they are a legacy of someone else's mistakes.

There are two schools of thought on training aids. One says that by their very nature, they should only be used by good riders – and that good riders do not need them. The other, more realistic view is that in the right hands they can play a useful role. The key words are that they must be in the *right hands*: used roughly or incorrectly, training aids can be instruments of torture.

If a horse has a sore back caused by a poorly fitting saddle, or is stiff behind because of an old injury that no longer hurts, but has had a permanent effect on his way of going, he will not carry himself in the round shape most riders aim for. Attempts to get him 'on the bit' may well lead to the horse becoming more uncomfortable and the rider becoming progressively frustrated.

Unless the root of the problem is recognised, the time will come when the rider decides that he needs help. The initial aim is usually to 'get his head down', so the horse is equipped with a pair of draw reins or something similar. The rider may well be able to use these to pull the horse's head down and in, but this will not encourage the horse to work from behind and thus come properly on the bit. As the original discomfort will remain, or even be worsened, the horse will start to look for other ways out and the rider will have a different repertoire of resistances to overcome.

That is the scenario which makes so many people condemn training aids. But there is another one: if we go back to draw reins, which are used (and abused) more than anything else, they can help to show a horse what you are asking him to do when all else fails. They should suggest, never force, and the horse should be rewarded as soon as he starts to do what you ask him to.

The question of when a piece of 'ordinary' tack becomes a gadget or training aid is very difficult to answer. Martingales are widely accepted, draw reins are not, yet both *should* be used to prevent the horse raising his head above the angle of control, not to force it down. One definition could be that a training aid is a piece of equipment over which the rider has more influence than the horse – but against that, some trainers believe a Market Harborough is more effective than draw reins simply because the horse's own actions have more effect than the rider's hands.

Everything we use when we ride a horse, from bits to martingales, should be an aid to communication rather than force. The same applies to training and if using one for a short time enables you to mend a communication breakdown, surely it must be a better alternative than fighting or getting frustrated with your horse.

There are four golden rules which should always apply to the use of training aids. The first is that they should only be used if you are sure the horse has no physical problems, such as those mentioned above.

The second is that they should only be used by riders who understand their use and can handle them accordingly – if you are not sure whether something would be of benefit in your case, or have never used it before, find someone accomplished in its use and work under their supervision until you are confident and competent alone.

The third is that any training aid should be a means to an end, not an end in itself. It should only be used in the short term; if you ride your horse in draw reins or a balancing rein all the time, you are getting nowhere.

Finally, introduce a training aid carefully and use it for very short periods – often only ten minutes – for the first few times, until the horse becomes accustomed to its action. With something such as a Market Harborough or balancing rein, fasten it loosely rather than tightly to begin with even if it seems ineffective. The horse will still be aware of its presence, and is more likely to accept its influence when you adjust it to its effective length.

Even if the horse accepts it and readily starts to work in a round shape, keep early sessions short and build up gradually. Imagine how you would feel if you were asked to exercise muscles you did not normally use: it does not take long for them to become tired, and the last thing you want is a sore and resentful horse.

Whatever you use, do not expect it to take the place of a correct schooling programme – though it may enhance it. Unfortunately, there is no such thing as a magic wand.

## Draw and running reins

Although these are often used as interchangeable terms, there is a difference. Draw reins start between the horse's front legs, then go through the bit rings and back to the rider's hands; running reins start at the girth under the saddle flaps, then also go through the bit rings and back to the rider's hands. Draw reins have a more definite effect and encourage the horse to lower his head, while running reins ask him to bring in his nose but not to lower his head so much.

*When the horse lowers his head in response to the action of the draw reins, it is important to 'give' with them as his reward.*

Although they are referred to as 'reins', they are actually one continuous rein with either loops or clips at the end. With the first design, the girth passes through the loops, while with the second the clips fasten to an attachment on the girth. The latter is more convenient, as you do not have to undo the girth to remove the draw reins – useful when warming up at a show.

Leather draw reins are rarely seen these days. Most people use cotton webbing, which is cheaper and nice to hold as long as it is substantial. Avoid nylon ones, they are cheapest of all but too light and flimsy; to be effective and run freely, the rein must have enough weight. Nylon is also unpleasant to hold, even if you wear gloves, and can burn and cut if you do not.

In both cases, the reins should usually be fitted so that they run from the inside of the bit rings to the outside – if used the other way round they have a squeezing action. Some people like to use draw reins for hacking out or warming up horses which tend to spook because it gives them more control. For safety's sake, put them through a neckstrap (which need be nothing more sophisticated than a spare stirrup leather) when hacking out. If the horse does take you by surprise, there is no risk of him putting a leg through them if they fall into loops. The safety of jumping with draw reins is debatable, though many people do it: passing them through a neckstrap would also minimise risks.

Draw reins are used a great deal by showjumpers, which is why many people criticise them (both the draw reins and the showjumpers). But the riders who are artists in their use – and the name which immediately comes to mind is David Broome – want their horses to go in a particular way, for a particular reason. A showjumper needs to be supple, rhythmic and powerful to cope with a course of big fences.

The power must be contained so the rider can position the horse exactly where he wants him and know that the horse will lengthen or shorten his stride the moment he is asked. The response to any aid must be immediate: any later is too late. By dressage standards, many showjumpers are overbent and behind the bit, but the driving force is still very much coming from the hind quarters. Watch the top riders warming up before a class and you will see that they work their horses on the flat in a deliberately overbent outline, to stretch the muscles of the topline.

Draw and running reins must always be used in conjuction with a direct rein to the bit – in other words, your ordinary snaffle rein. They should also always be used with a simple snaffle bit. If you use them with a pelham or double bridle you have overkill, and using them with a gag snaffle would lead to a contradictory action.

The usual way to hold the reins is as if they were those of a double bridle, with the direct rein as the snaffle rein and the draw rein as the curb. This means that the direct rein runs outside your little finger and the draw rein goes between the fourth and little fingers. Using them takes practice, so be cautious: remember you are asking the horse, not forcing him.

Start off by working the horse on a loose rein, with the draw reins knotted on his neck so they have no effect. Remember he needs to warm up his muscles before he can begin to use them. Once he has loosened up on both reins, take up the direct and draw reins so they are both the same length and use your legs to ride the horse forward into your hands. Some horses are so sensitive to the action of draw reins that they need to be ridden with the draw reins slightly looser than the direct one.

If he tries to evade the direct rein by raising his head too high, turning your wrists slightly and/or drawing back your little fingers will put pressure on the draw reins. As soon as you feel him give to their action, release the pressure on the draw reins so that you are riding only on the direct rein again. This is vital – it is your only way of rewarding the horse for doing what you have asked. If he gives to you, and you continue to keep pressure on the draw reins, he is going to wonder what on earth you want him to do.

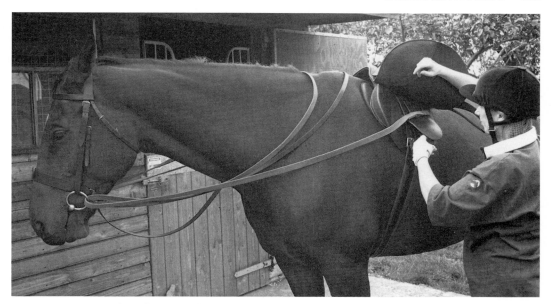

*Running reins attach under the saddle flaps and do not have as definite a downward action as draw reins.*

As long as you ride forwards rather than pulling the horse in with the reins, he should start to get the idea and put his back end underneath him, which in turn will lighten his forehand. Soon you should be able to warm up, work for a short time with the draw reins, then knot them on his neck and work him in the same framework with the direct rein alone. After a short period – usually four to six weeks, depending on the age of the horse, the nature of the problem, his natural way of going and so on – the occasional 'reminder' session should be enough.

Some trainers use draw reins on all horses, including those who have just been broken. This is not recommended unless your riding skills are on a par with those of David Broome; a horse cannot work in an outline until he has built up the muscle structure which enables him to do so. In the right hands, very short sessions to suggest a rounder shape may help him to do this, but in the wrong ones he will be made stiff and sore by the unaccustomed demands.

Draw reins can be very effective in showing older horses, who have worked long and flat, how you want them to go. A horse who has point-to-pointed, for example, may go forwards with great gusto but not have the faintest idea about working in a round frame. Used tactfully and for short periods, draw reins can help him achieve the right idea.

If a horse has a tendency to rear, do not use draw reins unless you are sure you will be able to release them immediately he starts to go up. There is a risk that if he manages to stand up, but cannot use his head and neck to balance himself because they are pulled in by draw reins, he will go over backwards.

An overhead draw rein, which has a centre buckle, is sometimes used to persuade horses who lean on or bore down on the bit to change their ways. With this fitting, the reins go over the poll, down the sides of the horse's face, through the bit rings and back to the rider's hands. Again, they must be used with a direct rein.

The idea is to give a lifting action to the bit, rather like a gag snaffle. Both may seem to have a contradictory action in that lifting the bit asks the horse to raise his head and poll pressure asks him to lower it, but the fact remains that they suit some horses and some riders. If it works, the theory behind it does not really matter – after all, according to theories of aerodynamics, the bumble bee should apparently not be able to fly!

If the horse you intend to use an overhead draw rein on is on its forehand and goes like a tank – as is often the case – his schooling programme must be devised to combat this, with half halts, transitions from one pace to another and changes of direction.

## The Market Harborough

The Market Harborough is best described as a cross between a martingale and a rein. It is often categorised as being severe, perhaps because it was originally designed to help control strong horses. However, it does not deserve such a reputation and in some cases is preferable to draw reins.

This is because it is operated by the horse rather than the rider, and as long as it is properly adjusted it comes into play only when the horse raises his head too high. As soon as this happens, it exerts a downward pressure on the bit – and when the horse gives to its action, the pressure stops and thus rewards him.

The Market Harborough fastens to the girth, like a martingale, then splits into two arms, usually made from rolled leather or cord, each with a small clip at the end. Each arm passes through a bit ring and the clips then fasten to small D-rings sewn on to specially made reins.

It must be adjusted loosely to start with. Once the horse gets the idea of the feel it produces it can, if necessary, be tightened so that the action is more definite – but it should never be so tight that there is constant downwards pressure on the bit.

The Market Harborough can usually be used safely on children's ponies if fitted carefully and the child is a competent rider. Some producers of show ponies use it to help build up a good topline on small ponies, which must be preferable to endless lungeing or being worked by adults who are too heavy for them.

## The de Gogue

The de Gogue is in some ways a relation of the Chambon, but while the Chambon should be used only for lungeing, the de Gogue can also be used when riding. There are two different fittings to take the various uses into account; both work on a system of poll pressure, bit pressure and running cords or straps.

*The Market Harborough should be fitted so that it only comes into play when the horse lifts his head to try and evade the action of the bit.*

In the lungeing position, the de Gogue looks similar to a Chambon and works in very much the same way. Some trainers believe that it allows more flexibility, because the cords start at the chest, run through rings at either side of a poll strap, then down the side of the horse's face back to the chest fastening instead of finishing at the bit. 'Everything flows more: there is no dead pressure' was how one Continental dressage trainer explained its use to me. Whether every user could operate a de Gogue with his finesse is another point altogether!

In the riding position, the cords run from the chest fastening (which as in the lungeing position, starts at the girth rather like a martingale), go through the poll strap rings, down the horse's face and through the bit rings. They then attach to a pair of reins – as with draw reins, it is best to have a second pair attached directly to the bit ring so that you can ride on one or the other.

In the hands of a skilled rider, the de Gogue allows for precise positioning of the horse's head and neck and can be used to supple and soften him.

## The Abbot-Davies Balancing Rein

When Major Peter Abbot-Davies first introduced his balancing rein in the 1970s, it sent shockwaves through the traditional horse world. A lot of people were ready to condemn it as cranky and even cruel without attempting to learn anything about its inventor's beliefs – mainly because its introduction involved linking the mouth to the tail.

This technique is one which goes back to the ancient Egyptians and enabled them to school their chariot horses to face a charging bull. Major Abbot-Davies believed that this showed the horse how much easier it was to work with his quarters underneath him, and said he never experienced any fear or resentment even from horses who had previously been difficult rides!

Once the horse had been ridden with the balancing rein adjusted in this way, its inventor switched to a more conventional adjustment. A lot of today's users skip the 'mouth to tail' work and the company which markets the balancing rein claims it is not essential. It works on a system of pulleys and looks quite formidable, but if you examine the components closely there is no element of force.

Major Abbot-Davies wrote an explanatory booklet which is still included in every balancing rein kit sold. In it, he says that if it is used every day it will strengthen the horse's back muscles rapidly. At first, it must only be used for a few minutes at a time or the horse's muscles may become stiff and sore.

He emphasises that the rider's legs must keep the horse working and his hands must be more mobile than usual to prevent the horse from leaning on the bit – the only way the horse can evade the action of the rein. With the rein on, the horse works in an overbent outline; it is claimed that if he is worked this way for three months, he will build up muscles to keep him in balance.

Exponents of the balancing rein claim that if used correctly, it can only do good – but if the rider is ineffective, the horse will not be harmed. All that will happen, they say, is it will have no effect.

## The Schoolmasta

The Schoolmasta was invented by a successful producer of show hunters, Hilary Janion, for use on her own horses. It aims to help solve the problems of horses and ponies who lean on the bit or try to pull, and works by ensuring that the horse pulls against itself rather than against the rider's hand.

*The Abbot-Davies balancing rein works on a pulley system and is not as formidable as it looks. This cob's bridle is more suitable for a hack or riding horse.*

There are two versions, one for riding and the other to be used with a breaking roller. The riding version includes a specially strengthened numnah with detachable pulley and reins with a rolled connecting strap. The reins clip to the bit and take the strain when the horse pulls or bears down; he pulls against himself, but does not meet a dead force he can lean against. Nor can he use his strength to pull the rider out of the saddle.

Because the pulley system means that the horse is able to bend and to move his head to the side, the Schoolmasta therefore offers the advantages of side reins without their rigidity, which can sometimes be a disadvantage. It can also be used to help introduce young or badly schooled horses to the idea of a sympathetic contact.

By breaking the vicious circle of a horse pulling at or leaning on the rider's hands and the rider pulling back at him, it can lead to improved balance from both. In theory, a well-schooled horse should not develop such bad habits – in practice, they sometimes do, especially when you get a combination of a small rider on a big horse.

# Chapter 12
## Caring for Tack

The golden rules when buying tack are to buy the best quality you can afford and look after it. With leather tack – in particular, bridlework – judging quality is sometimes quite difficult for the non-specialist. To the uninitiated, a brand new bridle in inferior leather may look a better buy than a second-hand, good quality one that has been well looked after and kept in good repair.

One clue is to look at the construction quality, from the quality of the sewing right down to the finish of the edging and the keepers. As a general rule, the better the work, the better the quality of the materials. Producing quality work takes time: time means money, and it would not be worth spending either on inferior materials. For instance, a bridle stitched with ten stitches to the inch will probably be made from better quality leather than one done with six to the inch – simply because ten stitches take longer to do!

Hand-stitched tack is more expensive than machine stitched because of the time factor. It can also be argued that hand stitching is safer: the saddler sews with two needles and ties a knot with every stitch, so each one can be pulled tight and is independent. With machine stitching, there is a top and bottom row of stitching just as with a domestic sewing machine. The stitches are not independent, and if one breaks, the rest are weakened and will eventually unravel.

It is impossible to get machine stitching as tight as hand stitching. Run your finger over a bridle that has been handmade by a craftsman and you should hardly be able to feel it.

Hand stitching is usually sewn in a groove. This gives another bonus because it should last longer: it does not stand proud of the leather, as happens with machine stitching, and is therefore less susceptible to abrasion. Threads used in modern sewing machines are often cotton polyester or braided threads impregnated with waxes. They are strong and rot resistant, but this type of stitching still needs checking regularly.

Leather is a natural product, and so are many of the things used in its manufacture – these include vegetable extracts, bark, leaves and fruit. It is made by treating animal hides so that they do not rot, but remain flexible, strong and comfortable for the horse – though obviously these qualities only last if the tack is well looked after.

Hair, fat and other unwanted materials are removed from the hide by scraping and the careful use of chemicals. Other chemicals, called tanning agents, are used to expel the water that exists naturally in a raw skin. Traditional tanning materials include oak galls and barks; in North America, boiled deer brains were a vital ingredient!

If the leather was simply tanned and left, it would go hard. It therefore has to be treated with oils and other materials to restore suppleness. Finally, the outside of the skin – called the grain surface – is treated to give it an attractive colour.

The leather used in saddle and harness making is usually cowhide, though other sorts are used for different purposes. Depending on what the saddler is making, they will choose leather from different parts of the hide.

*Butt leather* is the best on the hide and varies in thickness from 1.5mm to 4.5mm. It is used to make bridles and saddle flaps, with the best and thickest kept for bridle making.

*Shoulder leather* is usually accepted as second grade, but is still useful.

*Split leather* is cowhide split horizontally to provide soft leathers where tensile strength is unimportant, such as saddle panels. Sometimes the entire hard leather surface of the saddle will be covered with split leather to give a softer appearance and feel, without sacrificing strength.

*Pigskin* is hard wearing and resistant to abrasions, but does not have a good tear strength. It is often used to make hard wearing saddle seats.

*Rawhide* is very strong. It has a central strip which is tanned and stabilised.

*Buffalo hide* is flexible and strong, though is not as attractive as other leathers. It is usually chrome tanned and is often referred to as chrome leather. Legstraps on New Zealand rugs are often made from chrome leather.

*Suede leathers* have had the grain surface removed. They are popular for showing saddles because they look nice and give the rider more security, but do not wear as well as ordinary leather.

## Cleaning and safety checks

Cleaning tack comes very low down on most owners' lists of favourite occupations. Look on it as a chance to protect your investment and the safety of you and your horse and it might not seem so bad!

In an ideal world, tack would be taken to bits and cleaned meticulously every time it was used. In the days when everyone who owned horses employed grooms to look after them, such care was probably part of the daily routine – but nowadays, when most owners have to fit in the demands of horse care around those of work and family, it is the exception to the rule. If time is short and you have the choice between riding your horse and cleaning his tack, there are no prizes for guessing which seems more important.

Compromise can be successful. As long as you spend a couple of minutes checking your tack for safety every time you ride and another couple of basic hygiene steps afterwards, a once a week 'proper' clean will be adequate. The exception is if your tack gets muddy or wet or both: in this case, emergency first aid is a must.

Before you ride, make sure that any dried mud has been brushed off areas of your horse where tack will rest. If you leave it, it could cause rubs and irritations even though your tack is spotless. Shavings in his tail might look untidy, but will not do any harm if you are in a hurry: mud in the saddle or girth area might.

Safety checks are quick and easy, but could save a lot of heartache. The commonest danger areas are stitching, turns and anywhere metal rests on leather, such as the part of your stirrup leather which goes through the eye on the stirrup iron.

Stitching should be repaired at the first hint of wear – and this means that your safety checks must not be half-hearted. Pull hard: remember that stirrup leathers, etc have to take your weight and a lot of force. Stirrup leathers are a common problem area; bend the joints away from the stitching to reveal signs of wear.

Bridle stitching is also vulnerable, especially the sewn turns which secure the billets on the reins and cheek pieces. Check that the holes in the billet place covers have not become enlarged so that the billet itself is loose, or you could suddenly find yourself riding with one rein!

When carrying out your safety checks, do not forget the saddle tree (see Chapter 3). Also check the other vulnerable areas, in particular the girth straps – both for wear on the leather and at the attachment points. Girth straps used to be attached with webbing, which deteriorated with age. You may still find it on old saddles, in which case it is a good idea to replace it with modern nylon webbing.

Saddle stitching often wears at the point where the knee pad joins the flap, as the stirrup leathers are in constant contact, but this is unsightly rather than dangerous. Saddles covered in soft hide are vulnerable at the skirt and flap edges, where the rider is in contact with the sewn edge.

Girths have to take an enormous amount of stress. Leather girths look lovely and are comfortable for the horse if kept clean and supple, but are susceptible to wear. Look at the sewn turns, the stitching, the chapes (the pieces of leather which fasten the buckles to the girth ends) and check for wear at places where leather turns through a buckle.

Synthetic girths should be examined just as regularly. Look out for stitching coming undone and chapes starting to tear off.

Buckles create a weak link, which can cause a sudden break or wear on the leather. The crew hole, which allows the buckle tongue to go through, should be checked from the side to see if there is any wear on the leather turn which retains the buckle. Buckle holes make inevitable weak points and stress lines should be checked for cracking.

Modern buckles are made from stainless steel, but some may still have mild steel tongues. These may rust or break – remember that any rust on a buckle will damage leather.

Every time you ride, rinse the bit and make sure that the numnah or saddle cloth (if used) is aired or washed as necessary. These quick steps are necessary not only for your horse's health, but for his comfort.

It only takes a few seconds to rinse a bit. If you leave it, dried saliva and perhaps food

*One for the dustbin! The splits round the holes in this leather means it is too weak to be safe.*

will harden and could rub the soft skin at the corners of his mouth causing soreness. If his mouth is sore he will resist the bit: why cause unnecessary problems?

Likewise, dirty or wet numnahs can set up skin infections. They do not usually need to be washed every day, but do not let sweat and dirt build up. Wash them according to the manufacturers' instructions; in between washes, take the numnah off the saddle and let it dry if necessary.

Synthetic tack is quick and easy to clean – most can be wiped with a damp cloth or hosed off. Again, follow the manufacturers' instructions. Do not assume that just because some synthetic tack looks like leather, it should be treated in the same way; one manufacturer of synthetic saddles did such a good job on a new range that some people oiled them with leather dressing. It might have been a compliment to the saddles' aesthetic qualities, but it did not do them any good!

Leather tack takes rather more care to keep it looking and feeling good, but it will repay the effort. The exception to this is a new generation of waterproof leather, which is easy to look after – it only needs a wipe with a damp cloth – but is very expensive. It is just starting to be used on saddles, but must not be treated with conventional soaps, leather food or oils – always follow the manufacturers' instructions.

It most important to remember that 'ordinary' leather is skin, and as such needs cleaning and feeding. Traditionally, this was done by wiping off dirt with a damp cloth and then applying saddle soap, but some experts in leather technology now take a different approach.

They believe that cleaning and feeding leather are two separate processes which require separate products. They say that warm water alone is not enough to remove grease and dirt and that if you put traditional saddle soap over the top you are simply sealing in dirt and leaving a sticky layer on the surface. The logical way to care for tack, according to this school of thought, is to use a saddle soap that is a cleaning agent, followed by a leather food, rather than a soap which tries to clean and condition at the same time.

Whatever philosophy you follow, use warm water to remove dirt. Cold is useless and uncomfortable and hot is too harsh. Many people use sponges to clean the dirt from their tack, but grease on the underside (flesh) is removed most effectively with a facecloth. A sponge is still best for getting mud off the top side (grain) because anything abrasive – and that includes the mud itself – will scratch the leather. Persistent clumps of grease, known as 'jockeys' for some unknown reason, can be removed by gently using a *nylon* pan scourer. Alternatively, do what the old grooms did and get them off with a pad of horsehair saved when manes and tails are pulled.

Once the leather is clean, it needs feeding from the inside out; it is the underneath, flesh side that is important rather than the top grain surface. Some of the new leather foods are designed to be used as often as necessary, but beware of using traditional oils too often as they can rot stitching. Tack cleaning has become so high-tech that at least one manufacturer, ColeCraft, produces a leather food for areas which take a lot of stress, such as girth straps. This company also makes one which incorporates a slow release fly repellent, which is very useful on bridles in the summer.

If you are using a product for the first time, be careful. Leather food should only be applied to the flesh side, where it is easily absorbed, unless the manufacturers say otherwise. Some products actually dissolve the dyes used for saddles, particularly black ones. They then transfer themselves to the rider's clothes – a quick way to ruin your expensive beige breeches.

Glycerine saddle soap can be applied to both sides of the leather, though again it is the flesh side which absorbs the conditioning agents. To be effective, the sponge must be damp rather than wet – you do not want the soap to lather. The traditional approach is to spit on your bar of saddle soap and then rub the sponge on it, but this is neither hygienic or socially acceptable in many circles! Either drip a few drops of water on to the soap or dip the end of the bar, shaking off any excess.

Saddle soap lodges in strap holes, where it traps dirt, so poke them through with a matchstick or clean nail. Old leather that has been cleaned frequently and regularly with glycerine saddle soap does take on a soft gleam, but this is probably more to do with actual wear than with the saddle soap. Do not use boot polish on the outside of your tack to try and make it shine: it will, but it will also encourage it to dry out and crack even if the flesh side is treated with leather food.

Boot polish will also make the tack feel hard and slippery, which is the last thing you want. Tack should be soft and supple, but getting it that way takes time. If you buy a new pair of leather reins, use a technique called 'lasting' which is apparently employed in the Royal Mews: hang them up for a few days before you use them and work a good glycerine saddle soap into them with your hands several times a day. They will soon feel much softer and nicer to hold.

Suede areas should not be treated with leather dressings or saddle soap. Brush them with a clean, dry nail brush – a suede brush with wire bristles can be used very occasionally, but is too harsh to use as a matter of routine.

As a general rule, try not to get your leather any wetter than you have to. However, if a bridle gets really muddy the only way to clean it is often to immerse it in a bucket of water and wash off the mud. If the water contains one of the new generation of soaps, this will be more effective. Use a nail brush to remove the dirt, as gently as possible, and wipe off excess water immediately.

Wet tack – including leather that has been made soggy by heavy rain – should always be dried carefully. The best way is to take it indoors and let it dry at room temperature; most outside tack rooms are prone to damp and cold and are, quite honestly, the worst possible places in which to keep leather! Never put wet tack in front of a direct heat source, even a radiator, or it will dry out too quickly and become brittle.

Store your tack carefully. Saddles should be kept on saddle racks or saddle horses to keep their shapes; for the same reason, bridles should be hung from bridle racks rather than ordinary hooks. A cheap bridle rack can be made by nailing a suitable sized round tin to the wall.

If leather gets damp, it is susceptible to mould. Fungicide is applied to leather during the tanning process, but eventually its efficiency is lost. You can now buy at least one leather care product to replace the lost fungicide; it is designed to be used once a year and should be applied to scrupulously clean leather.

If the mould growth is recent, you may be able to remove it and rehabilitate the leather. Never brush off mould growth in a confined space, as breathing in the spores is potentially harmful. Do it outside, then clean and feed the leather and check that neither the leather nor the stitching shows signs of damage.

Bits and stirrup irons can be washed and dried with a soft cloth. If you dip them in hot, clean water for a final rinse and then immediately dry and polish them with a clean cloth, you will get a nice shine. Metal polish should be used sparingly and with great care: never use it on bits, because you do not want any tiny residue getting into the horse's mouth, and do not get it on leather.

If your taste runs to brass clincher browbands – which really belong only on driving horses – applying brass polish on a cotton wool bud is the easiest way to keep it where it should be. Velvet-covered browbands, often used on hacks and some show ponies, are the worst thing in the world to keep clean. Many showing people make cotton covers for them which fasten with Velcro, and keep these on the bridle until just before they go in the ring.

# Index